This notebook belongs to:

Name: _____

Email: _____

Phone: _____

CONTENT

Pages	Topic

Pages	Topic
Pages	Topic

Pages	Topic
Pages	Topic

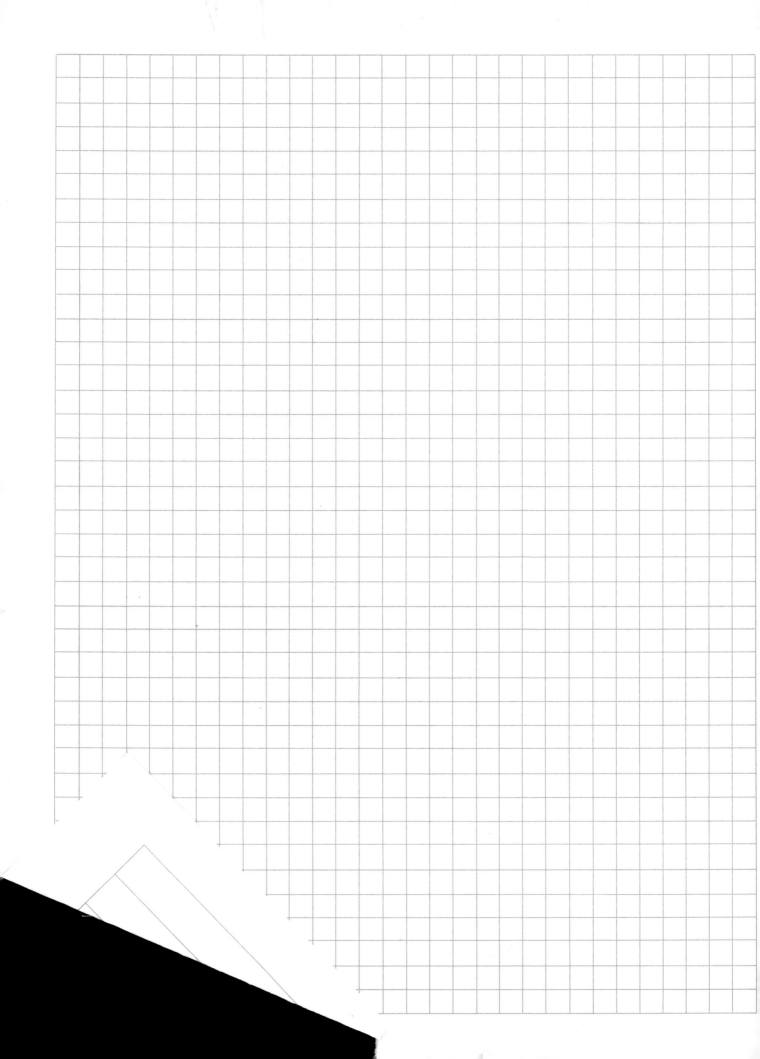

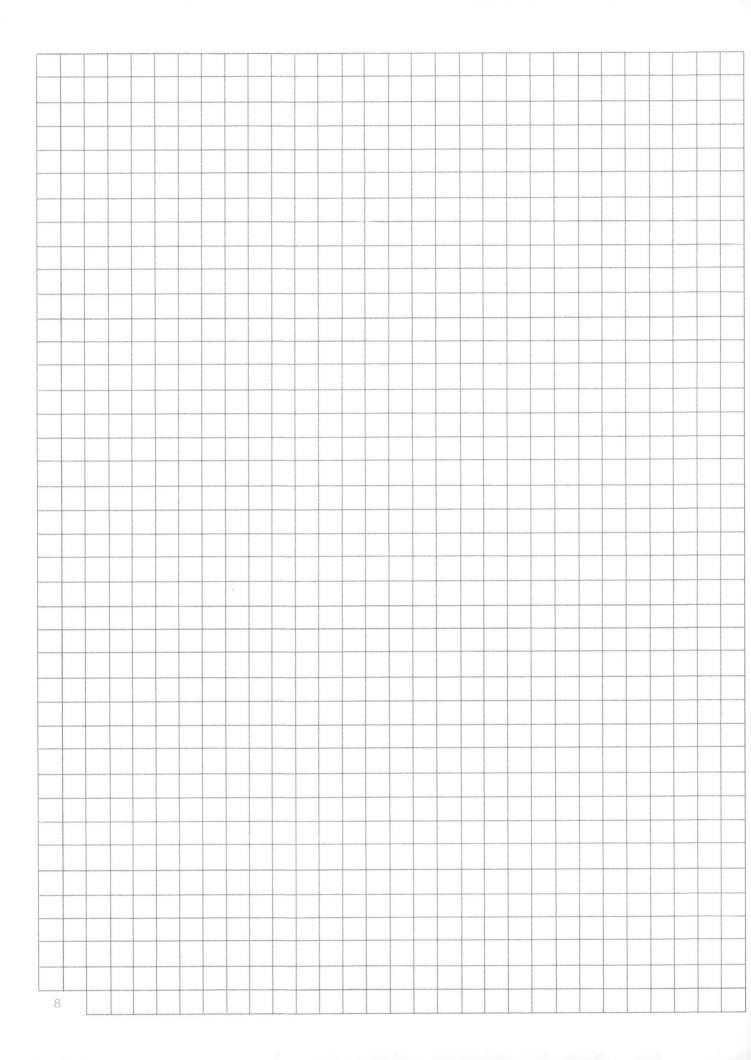

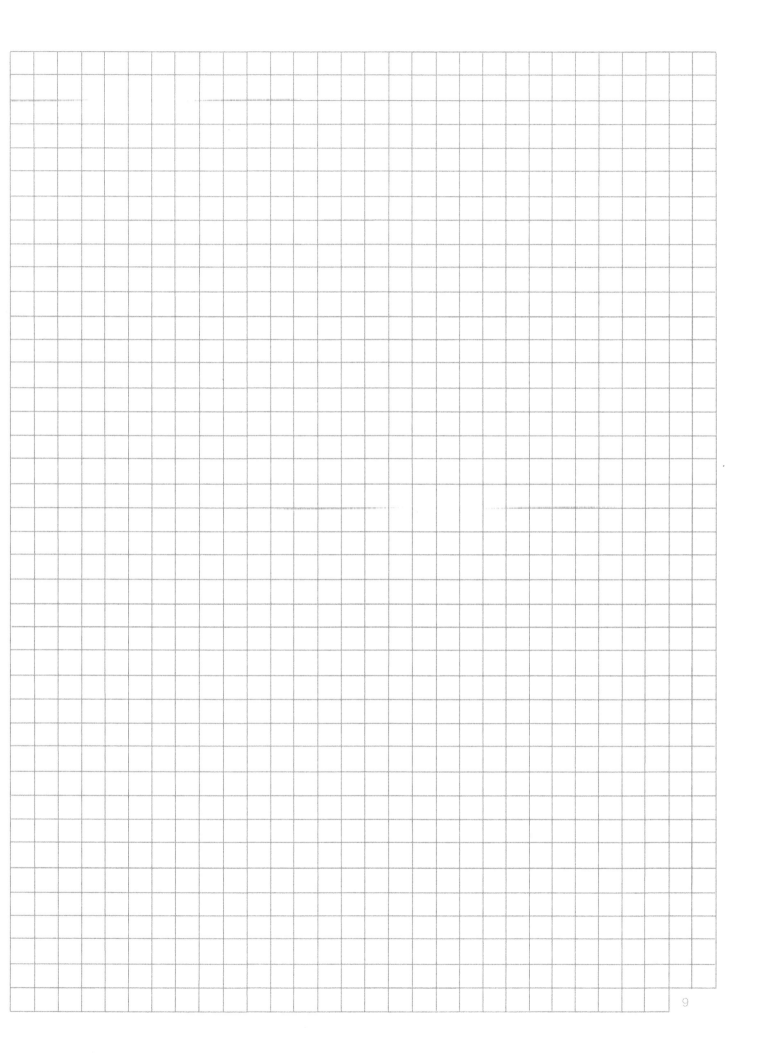

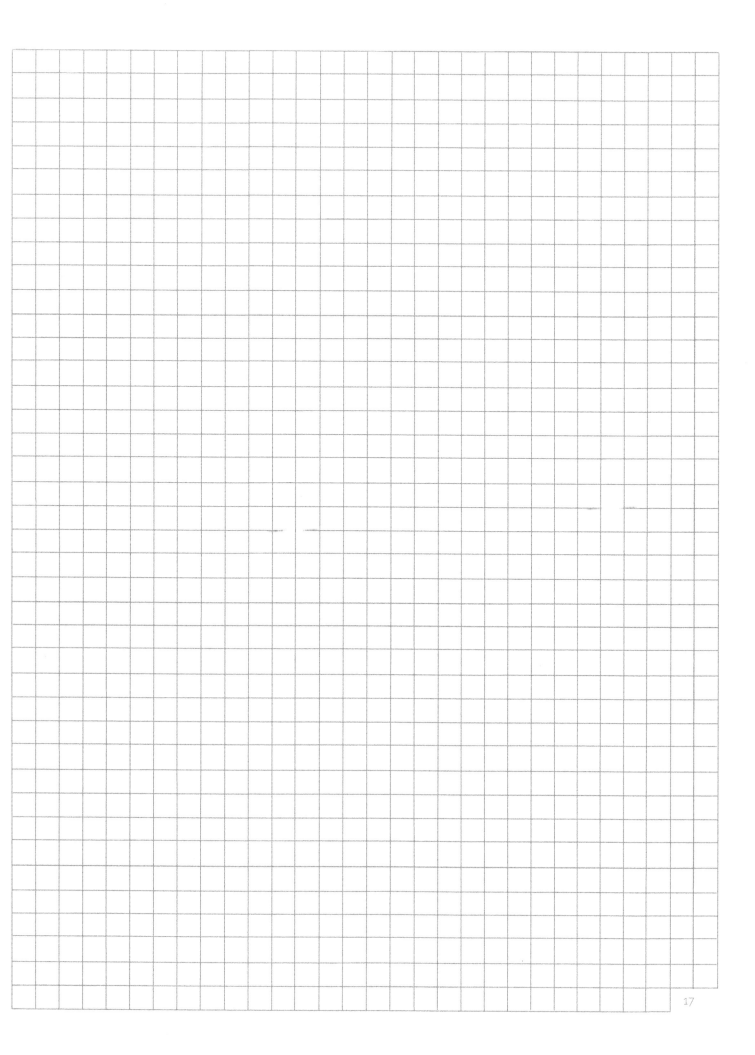

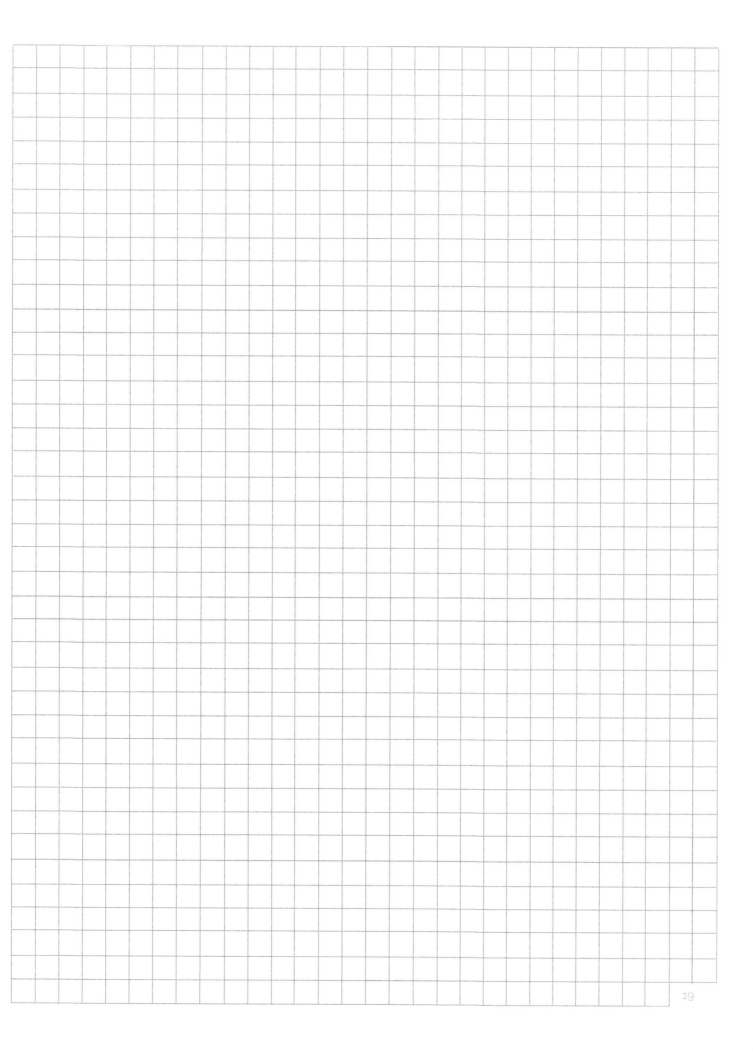

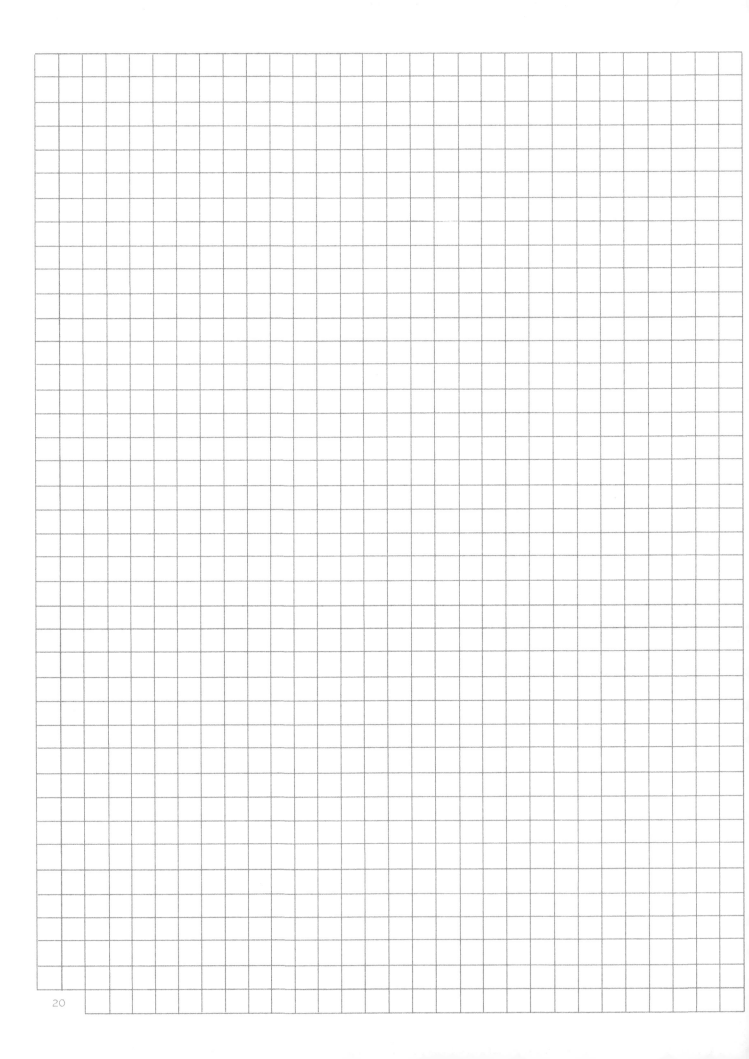

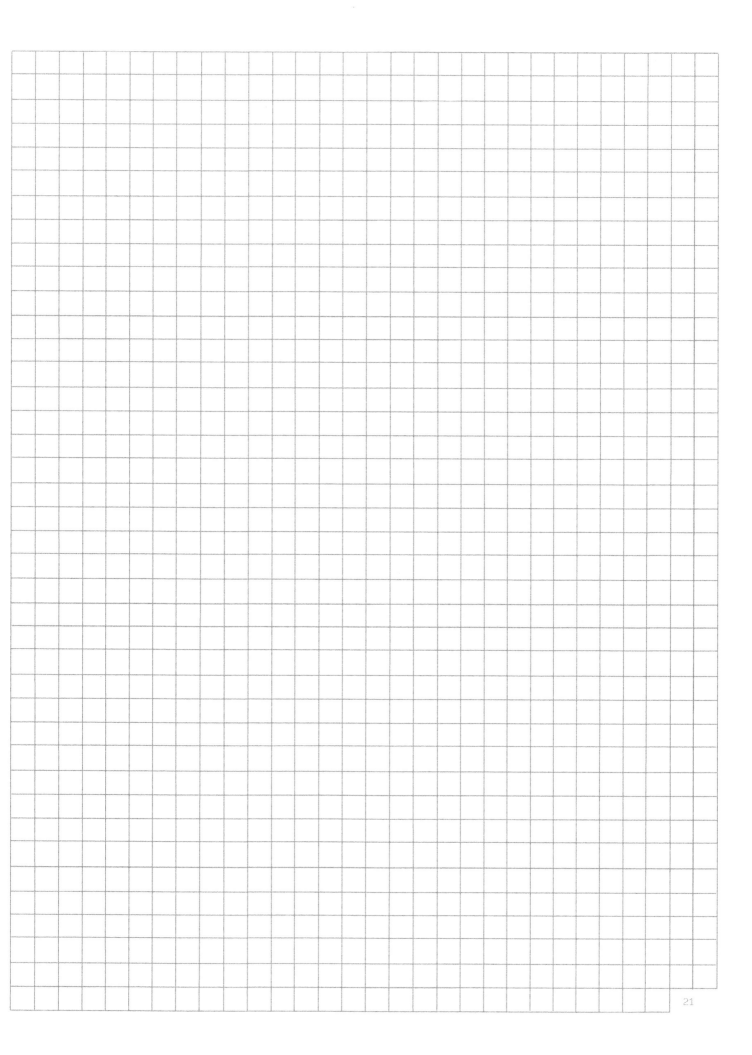

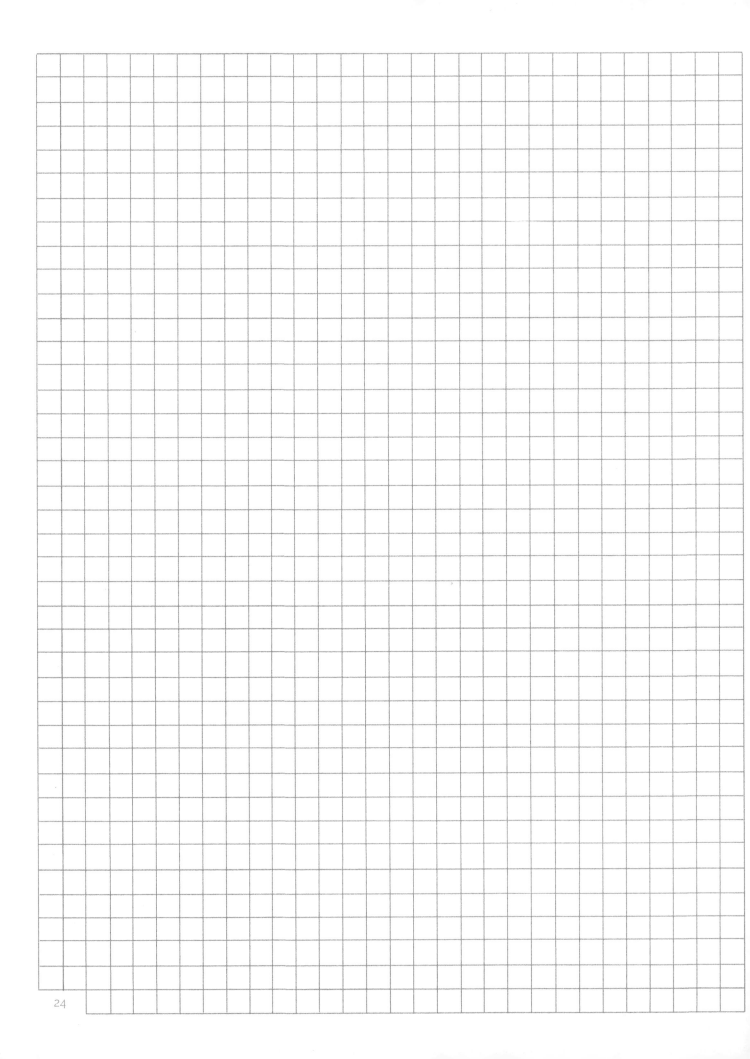

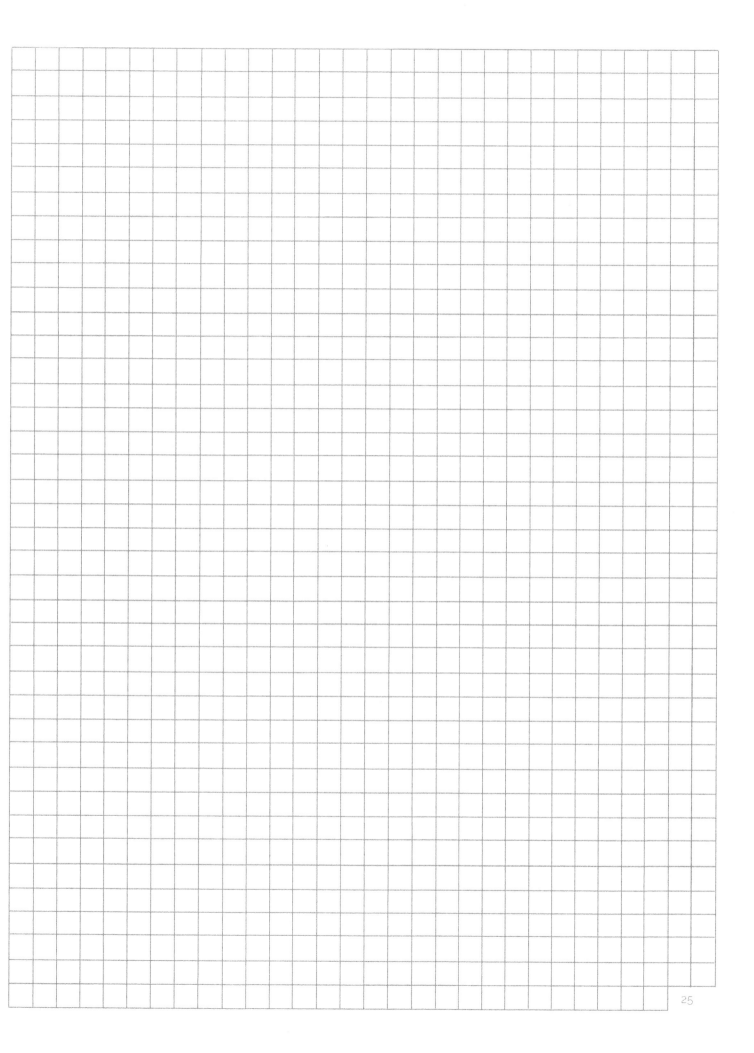

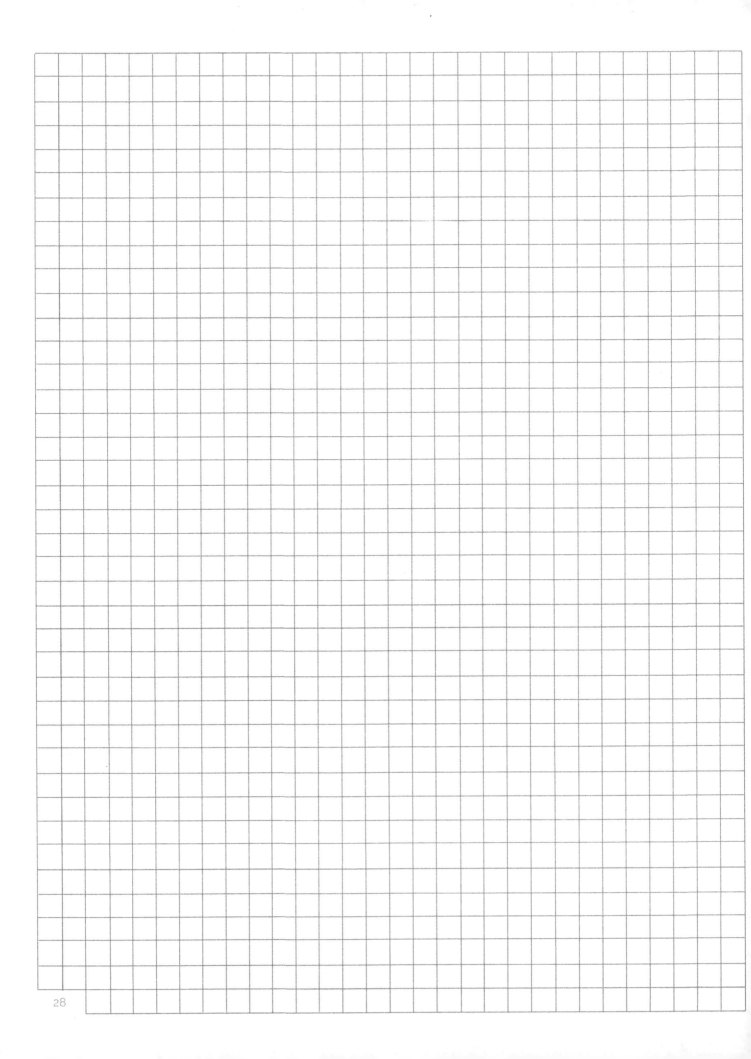

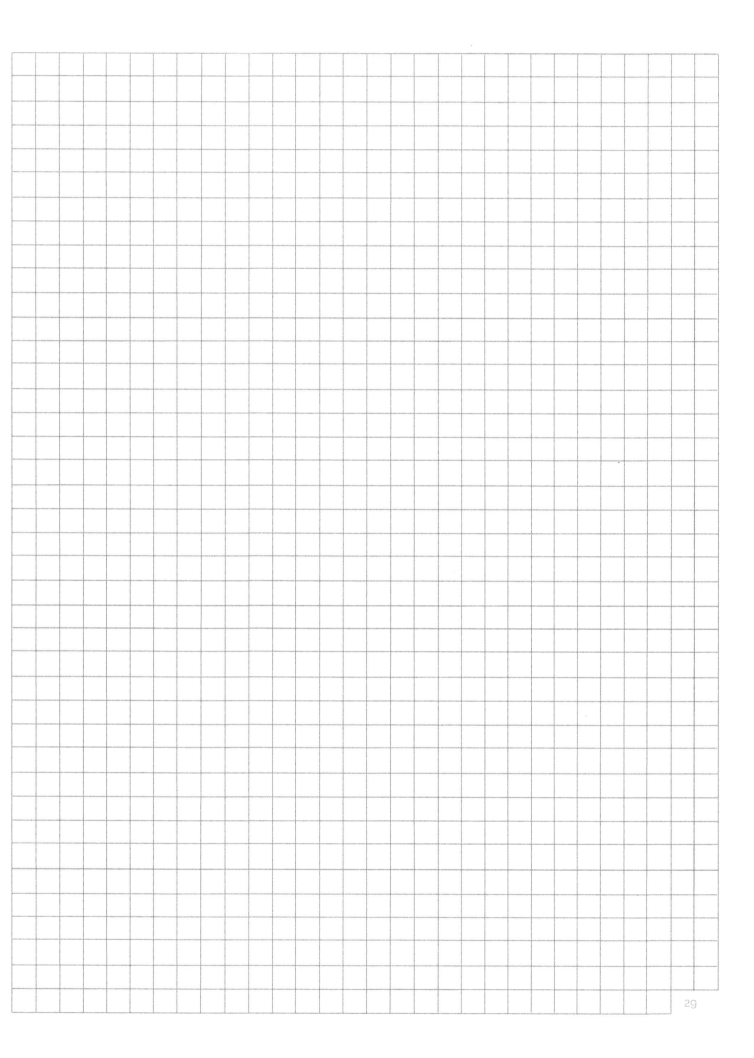

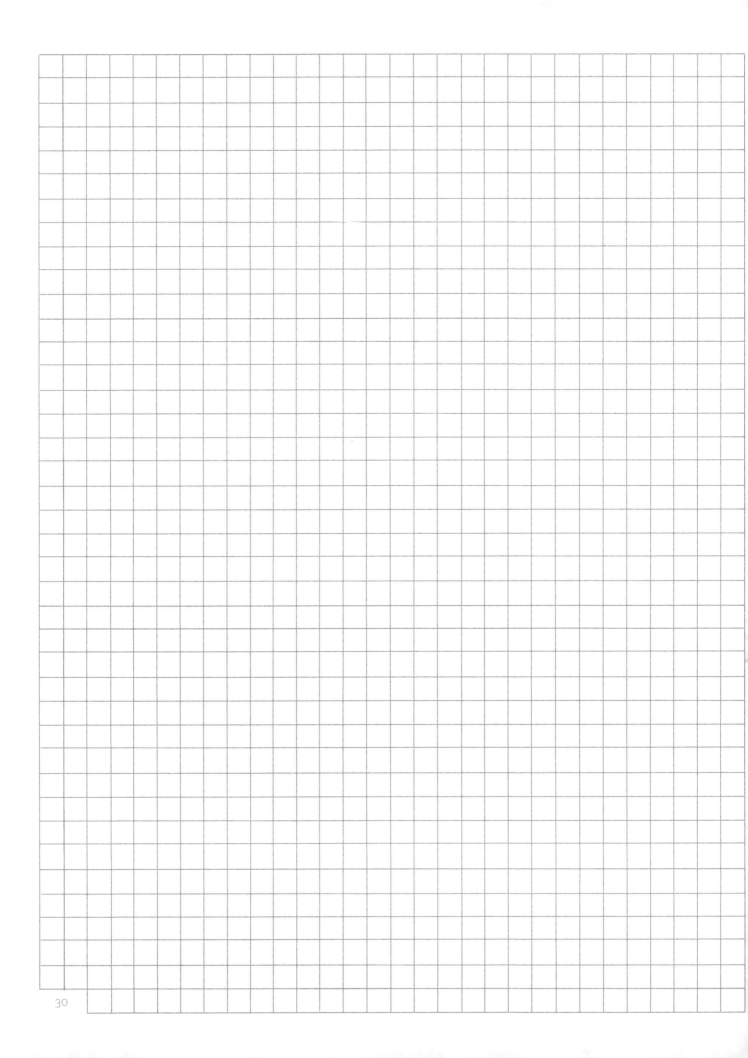

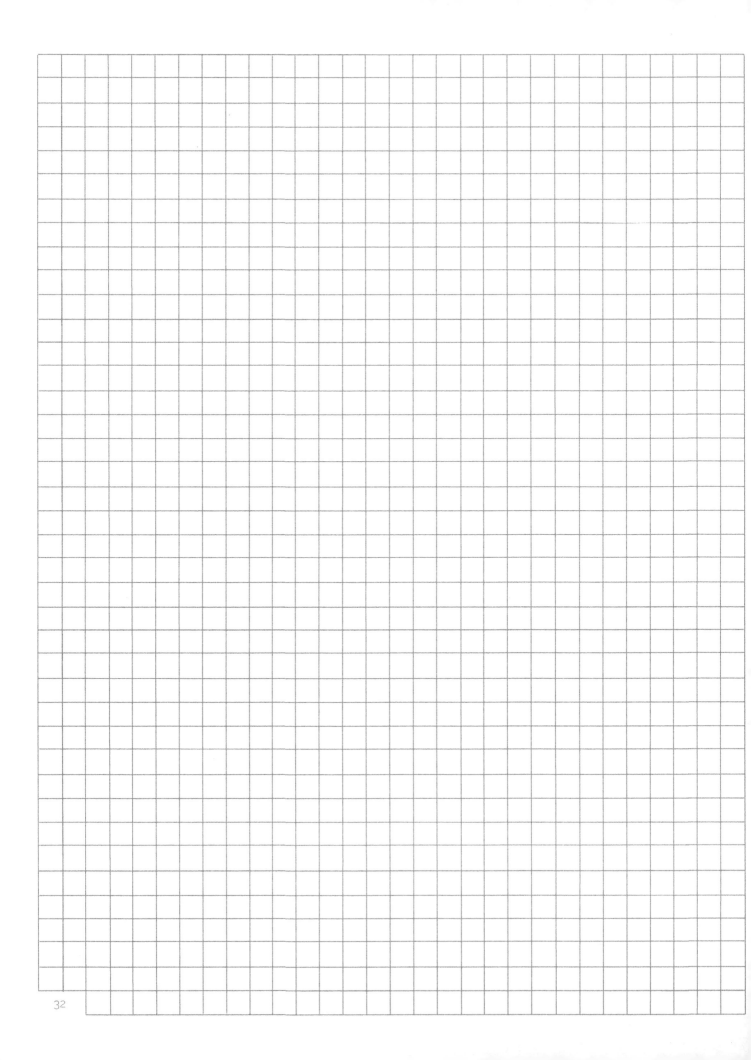

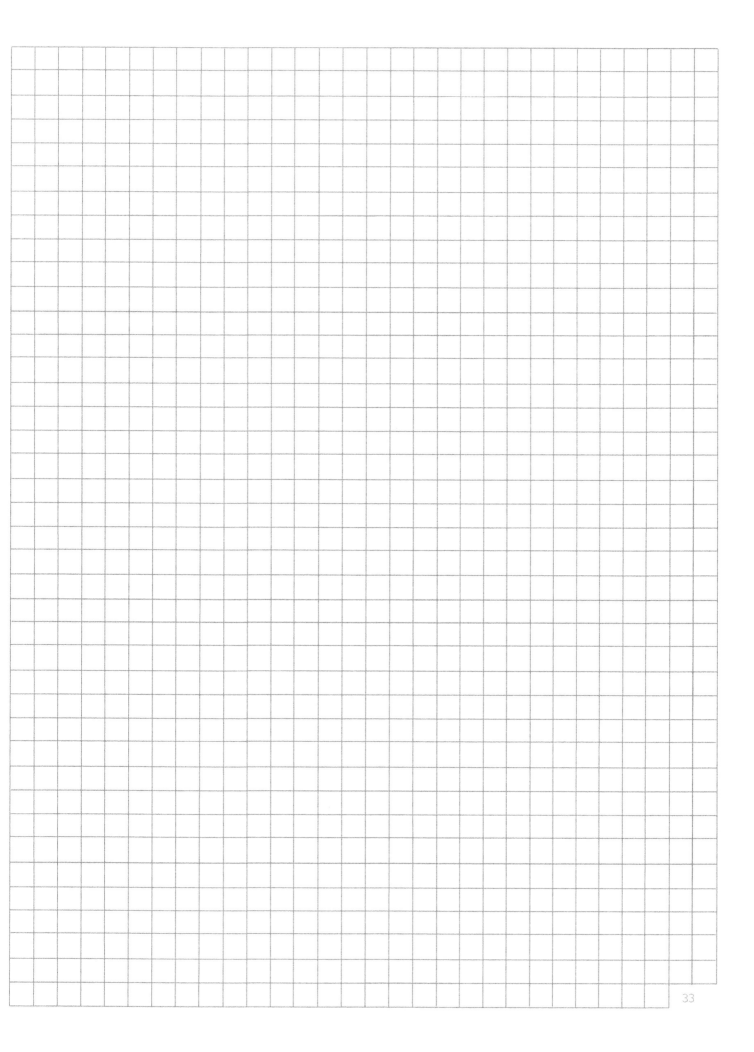

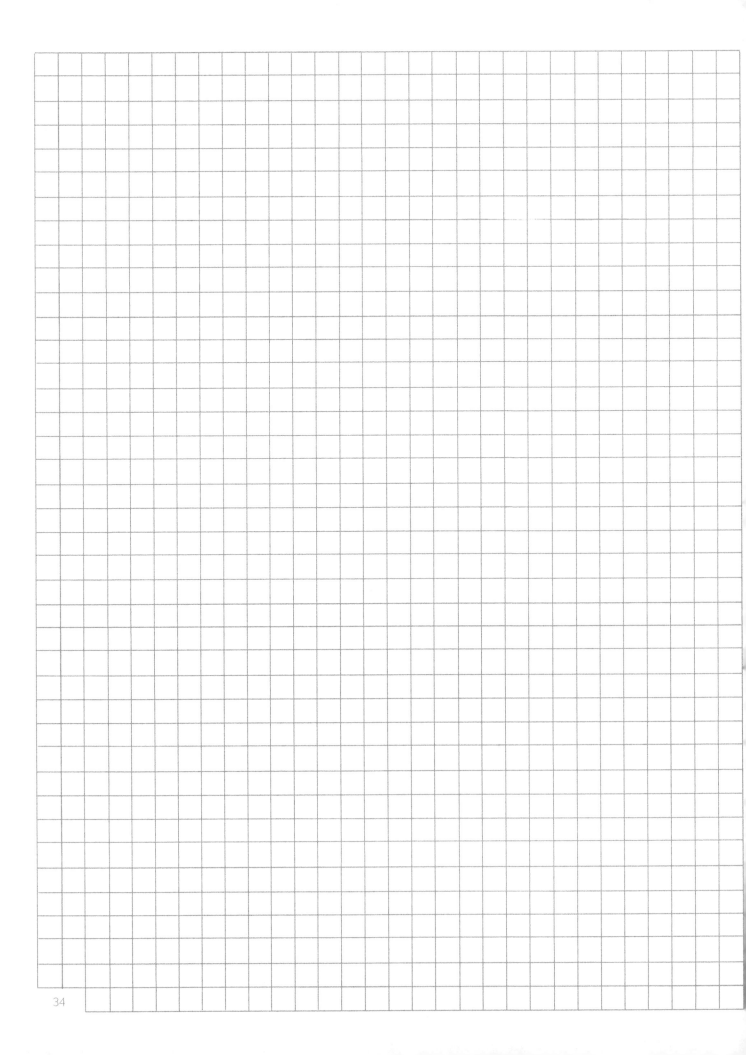

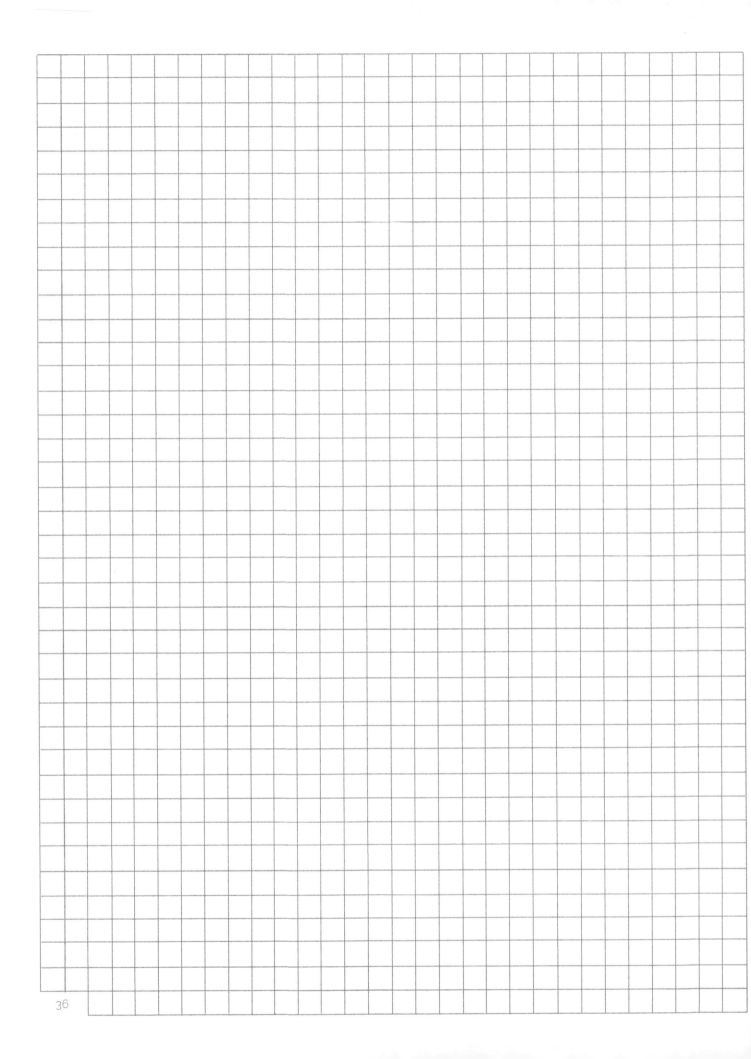

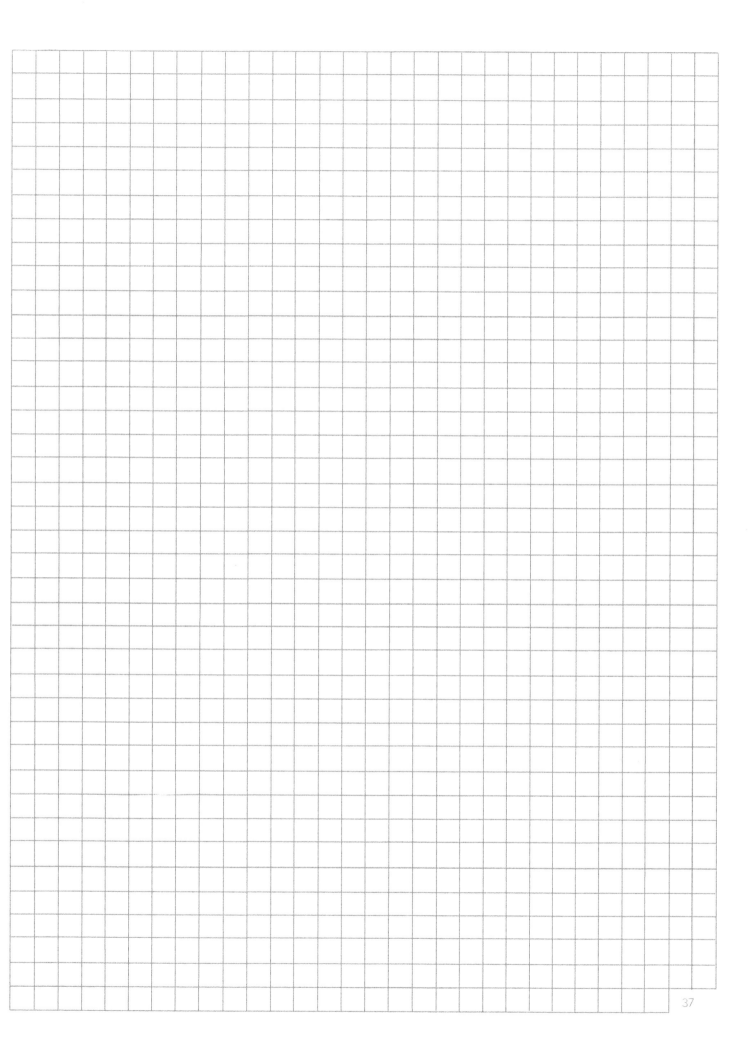

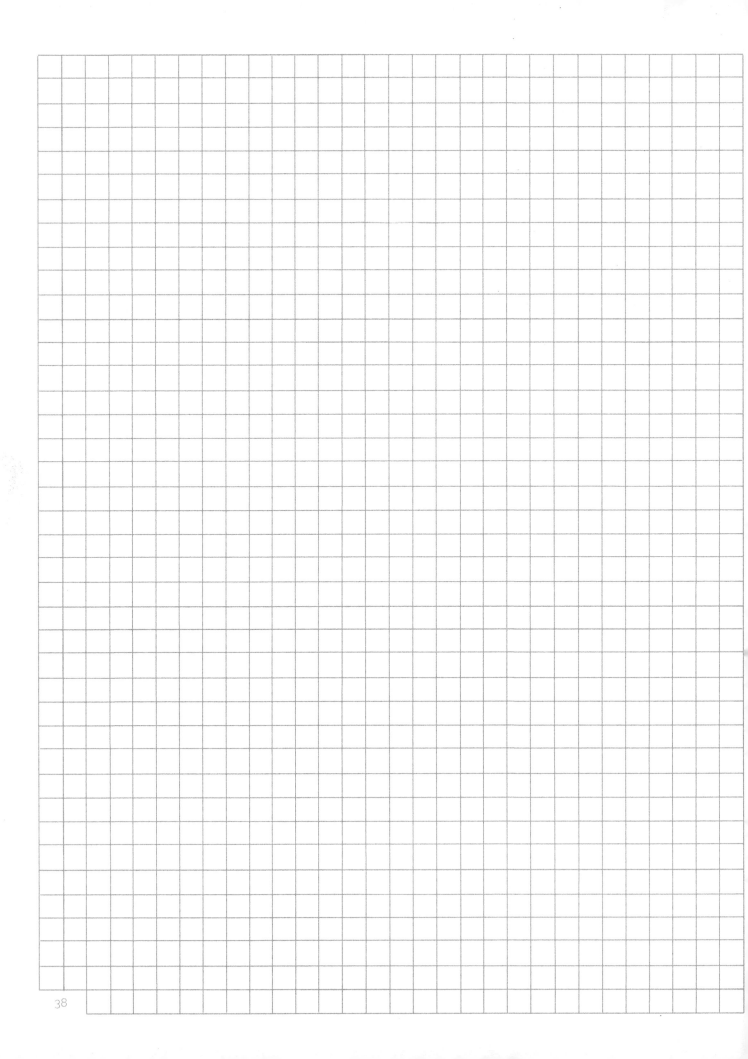

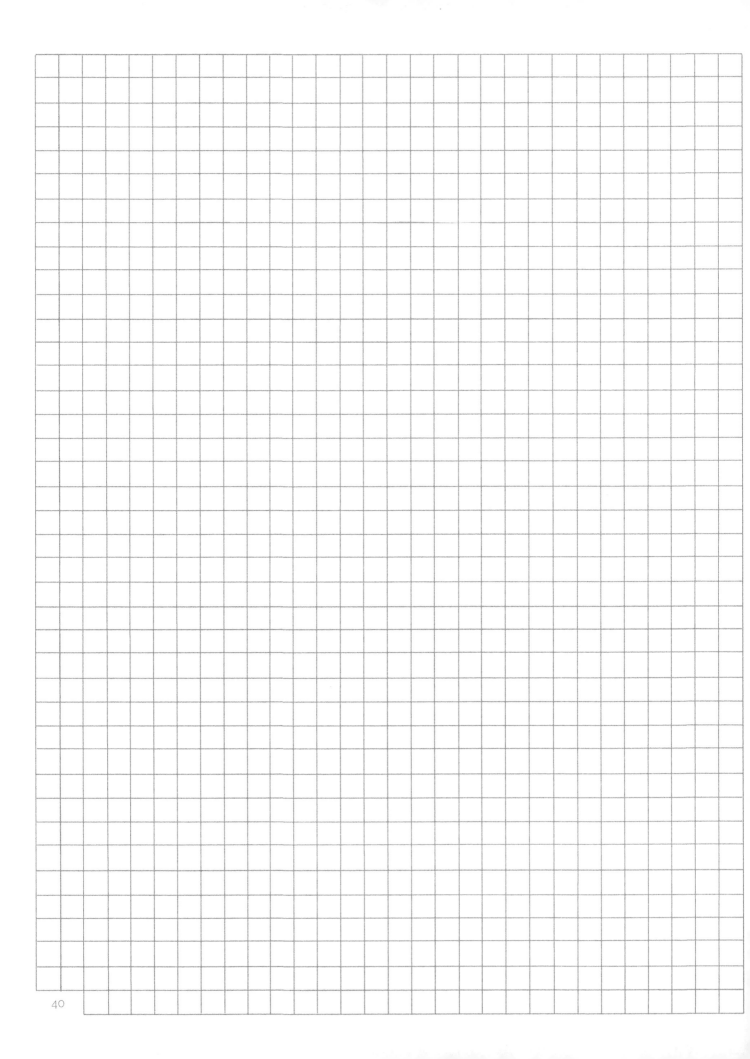

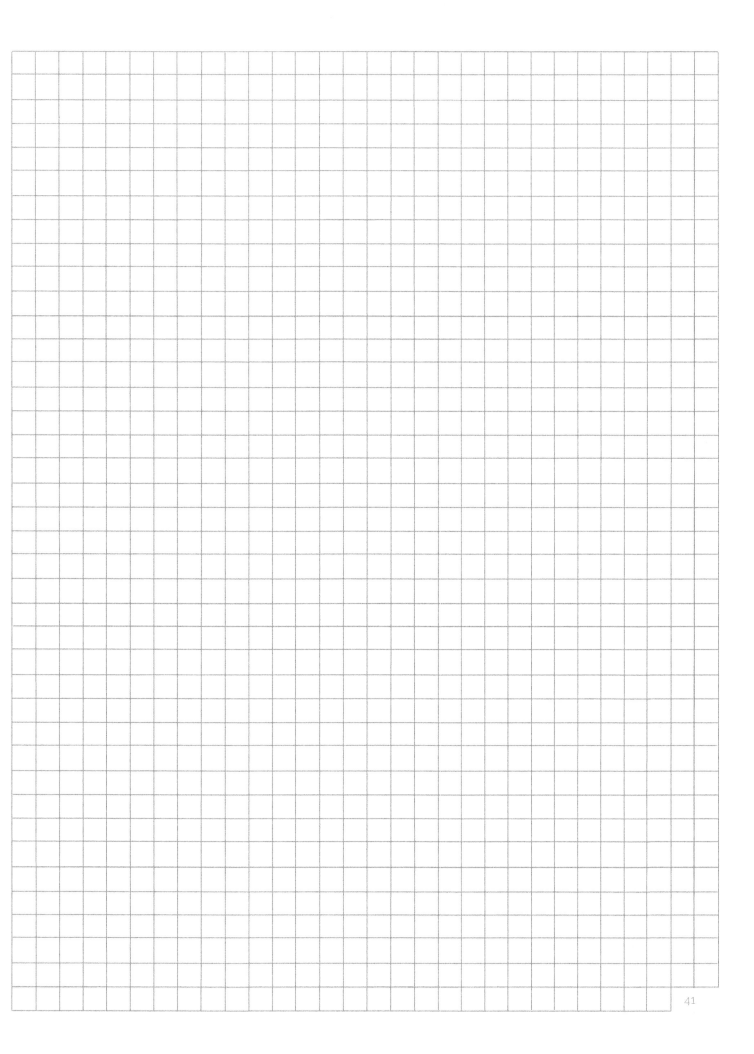

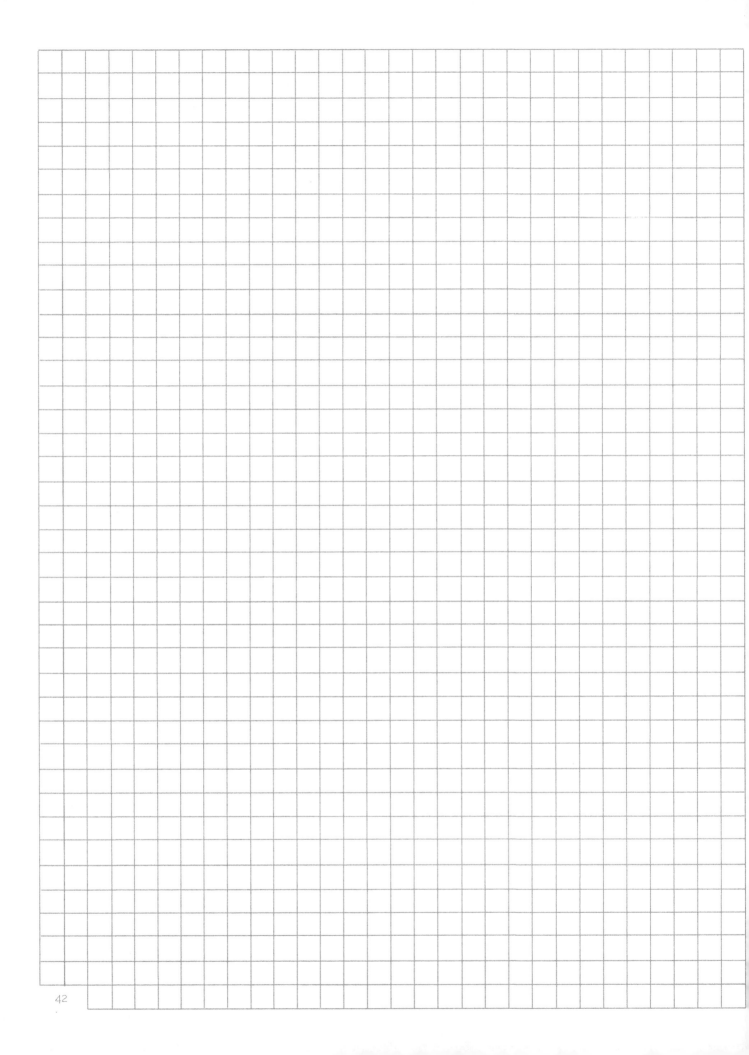

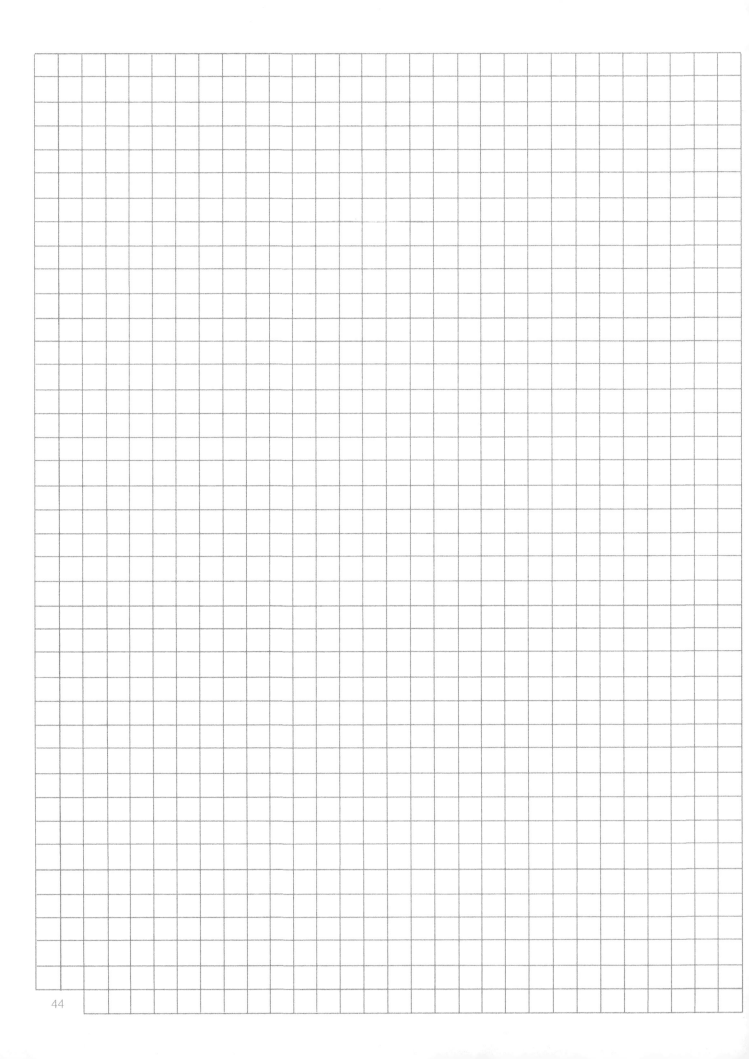

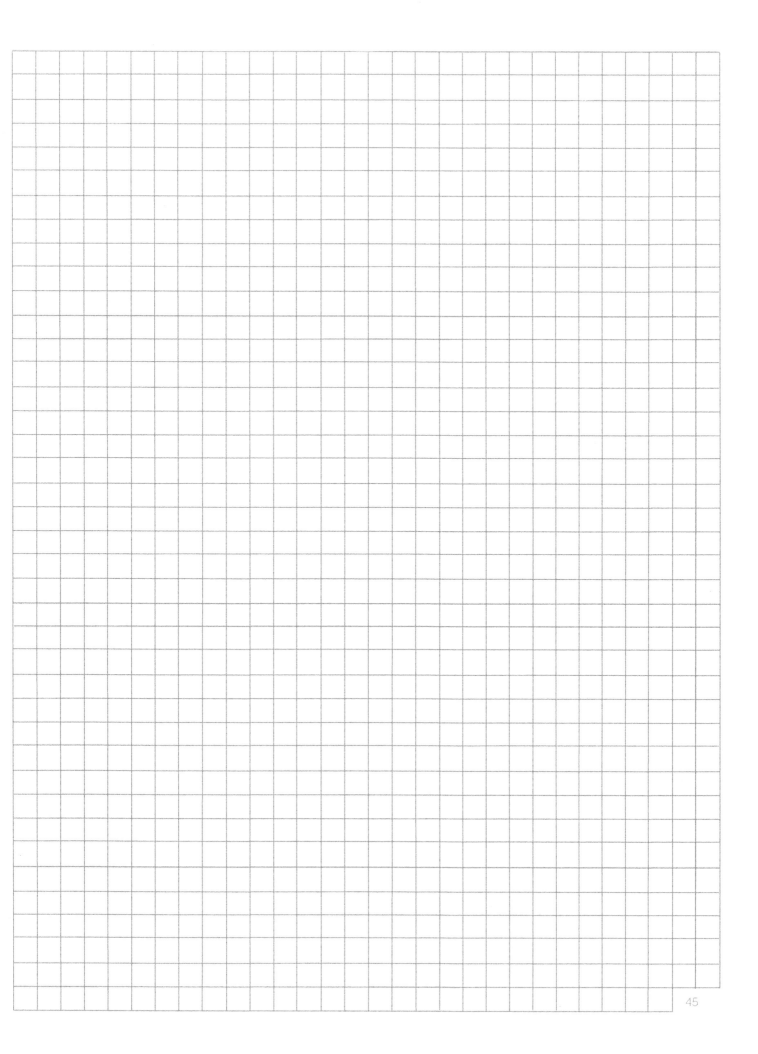

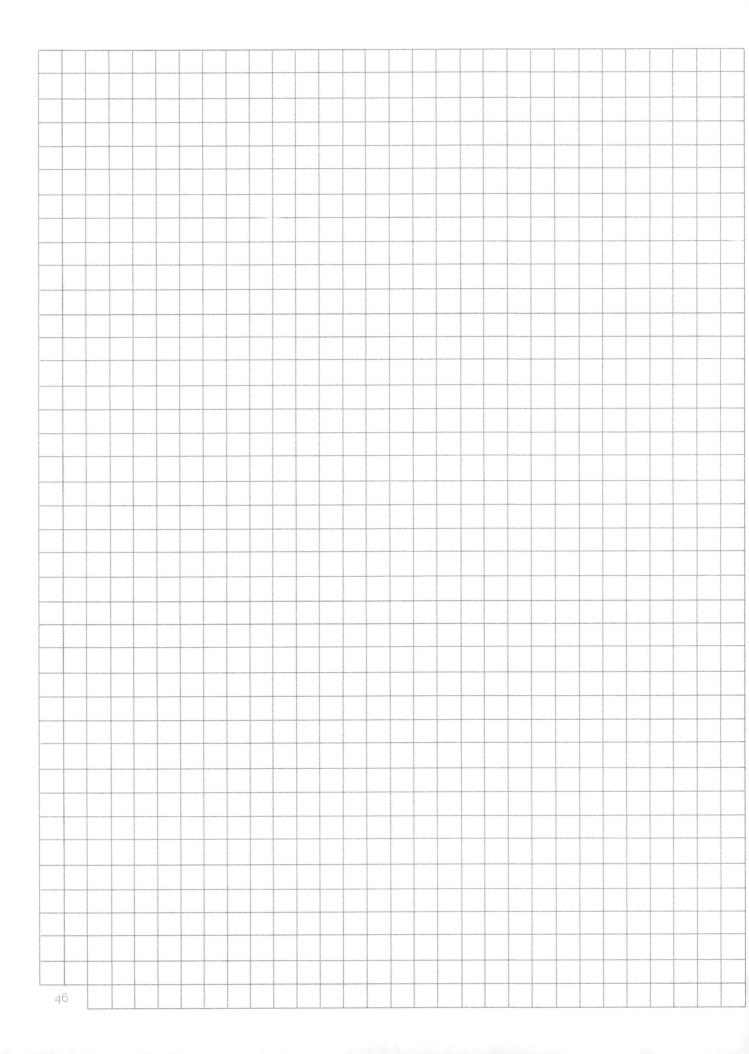

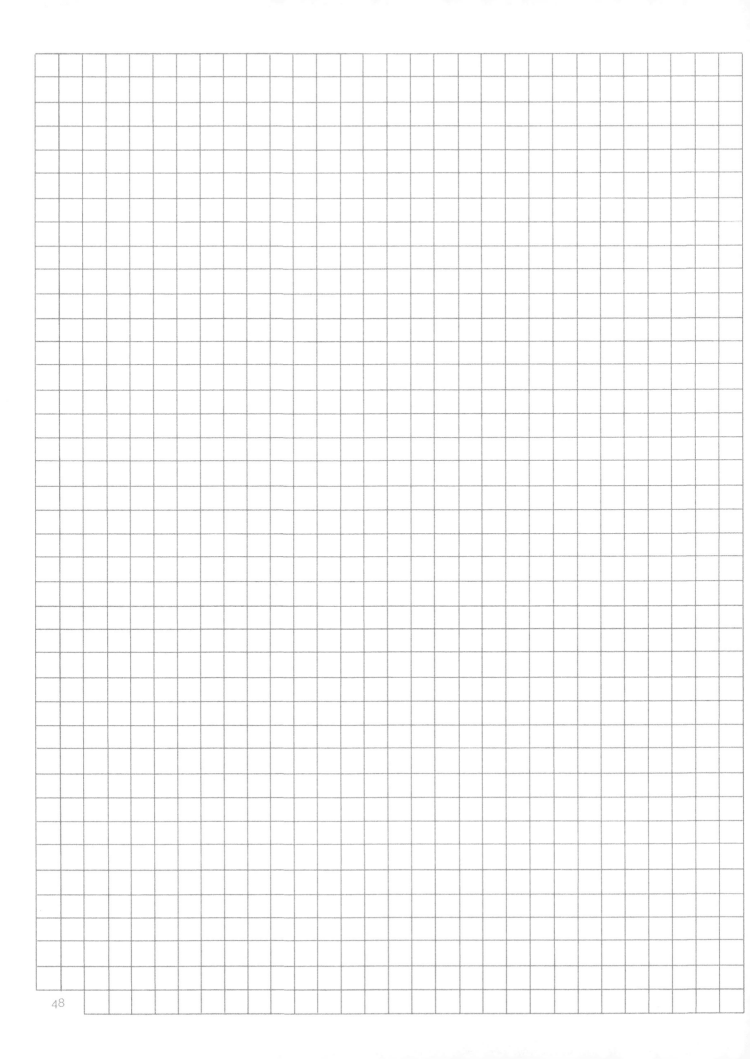

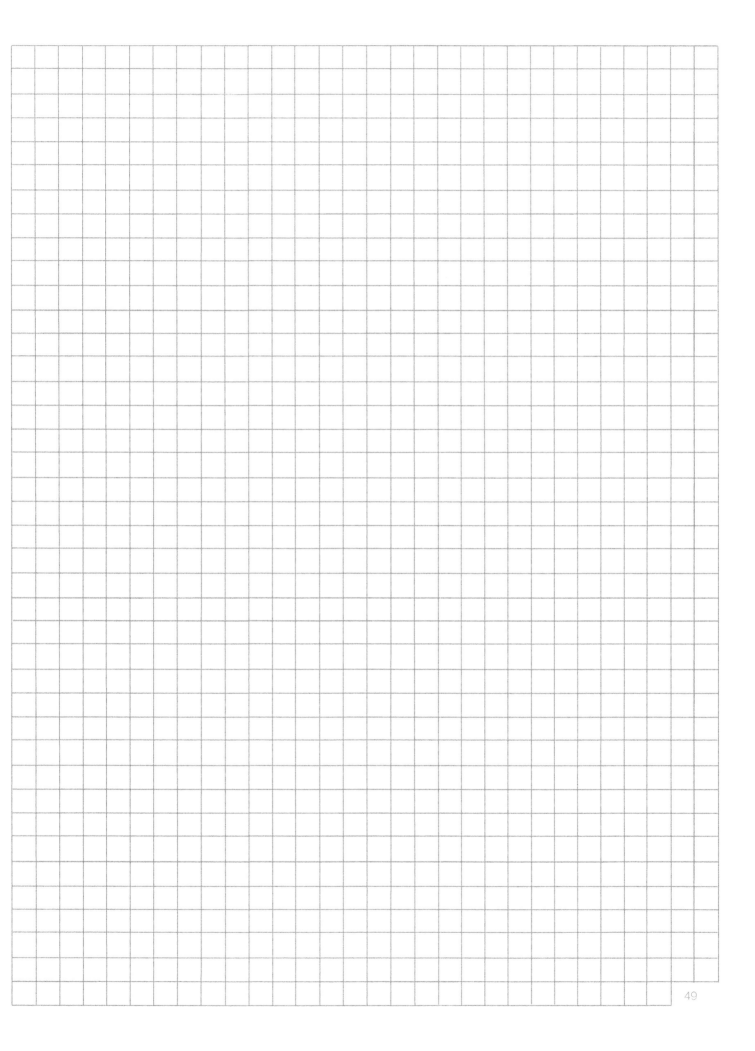

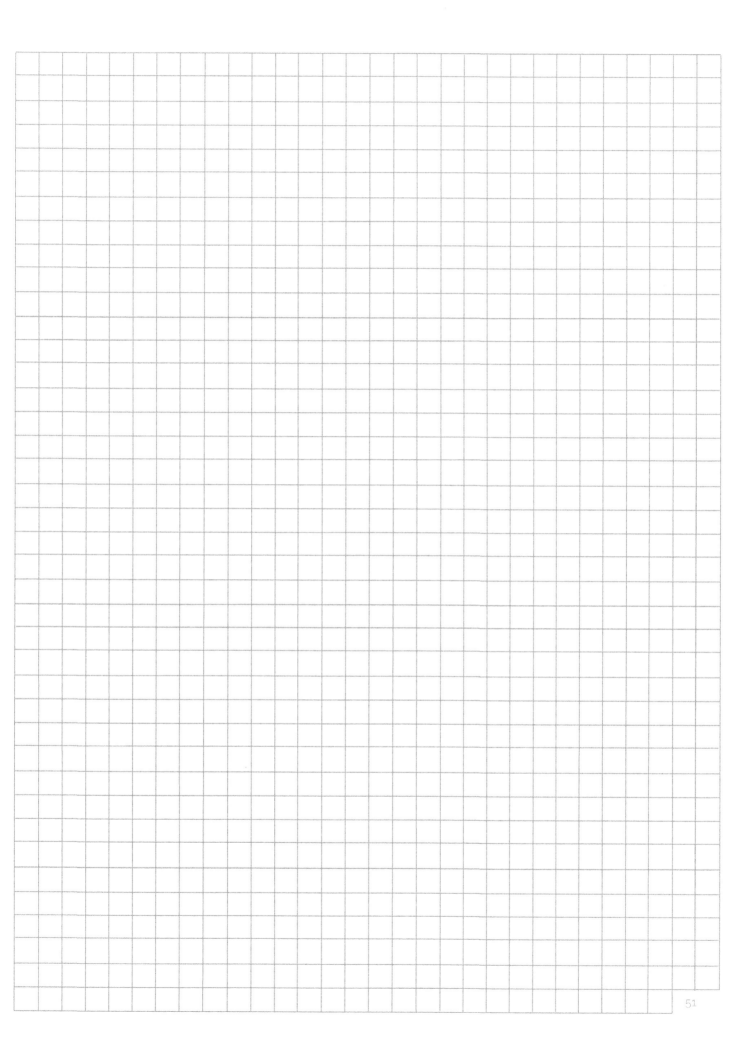

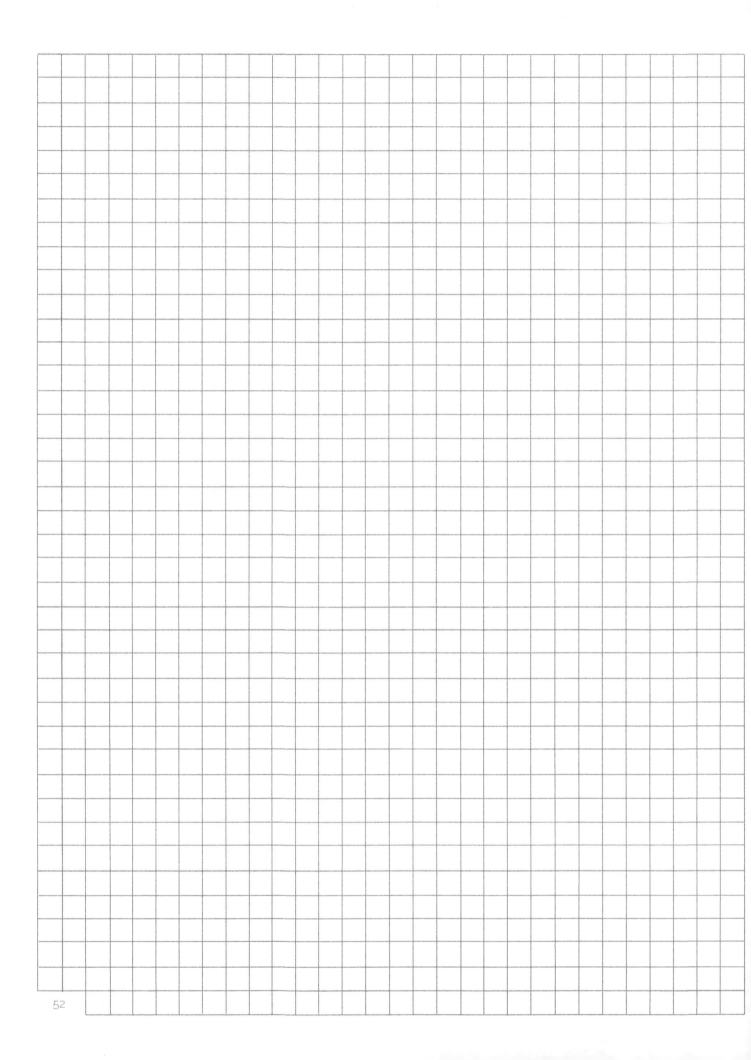

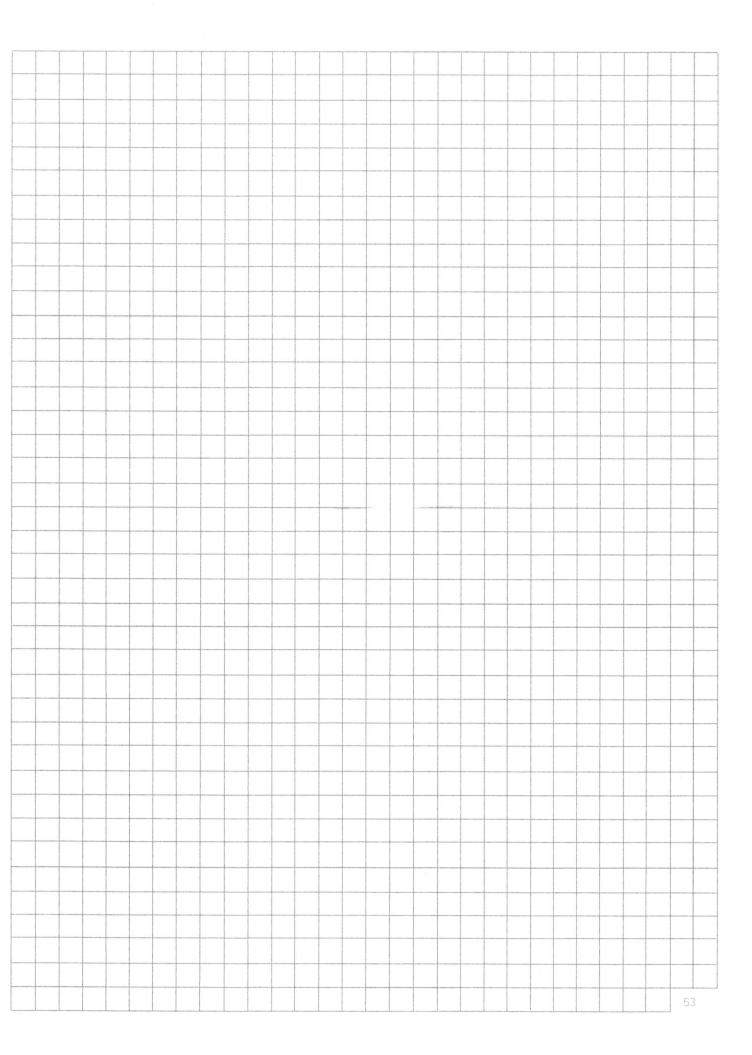

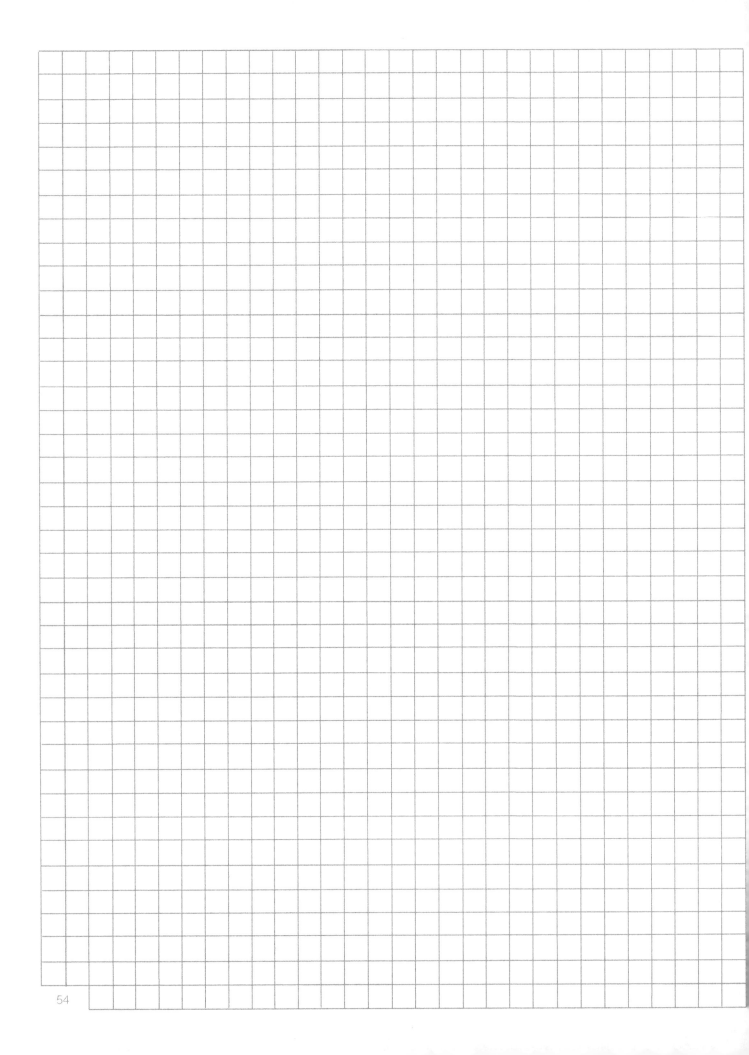

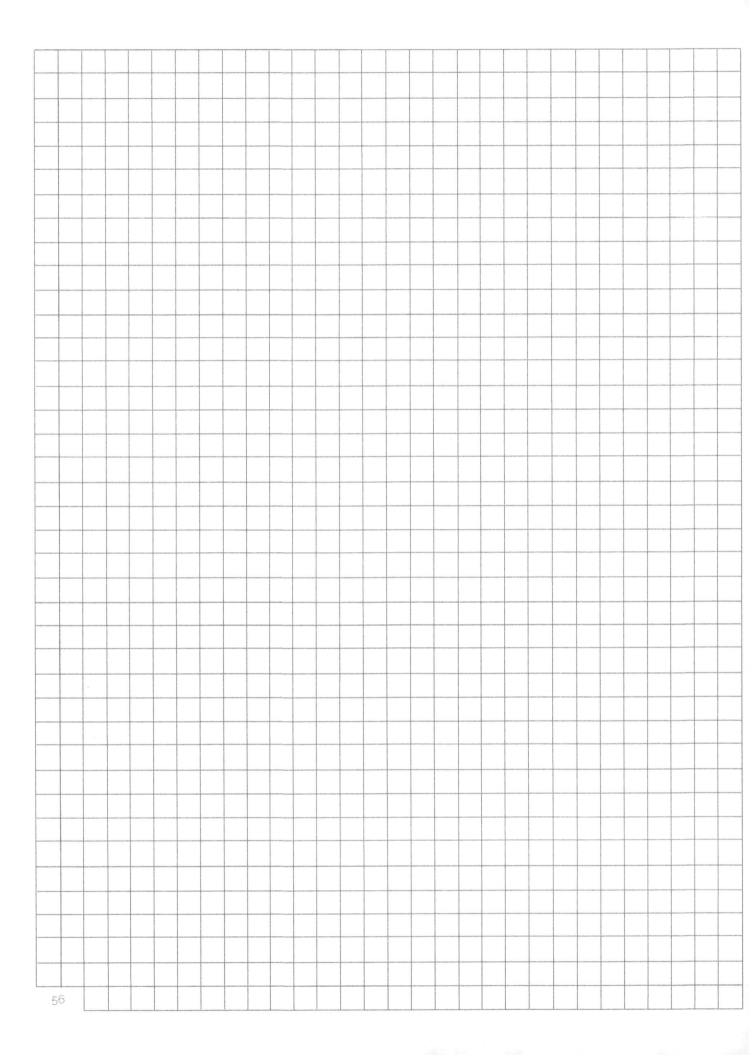

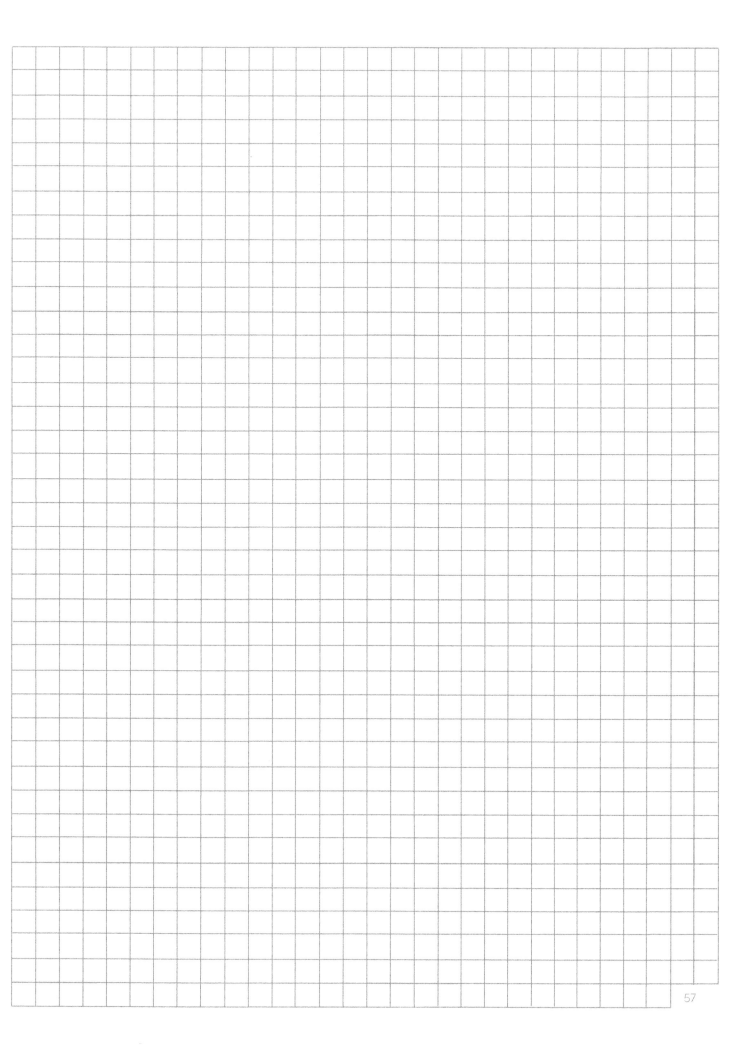

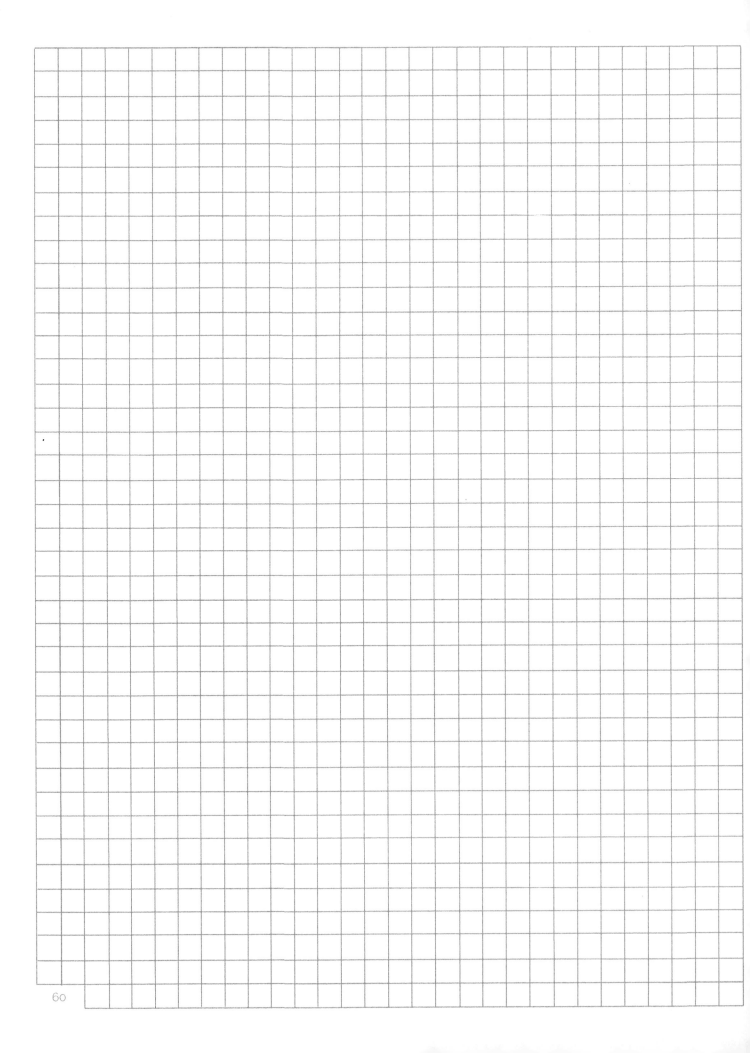

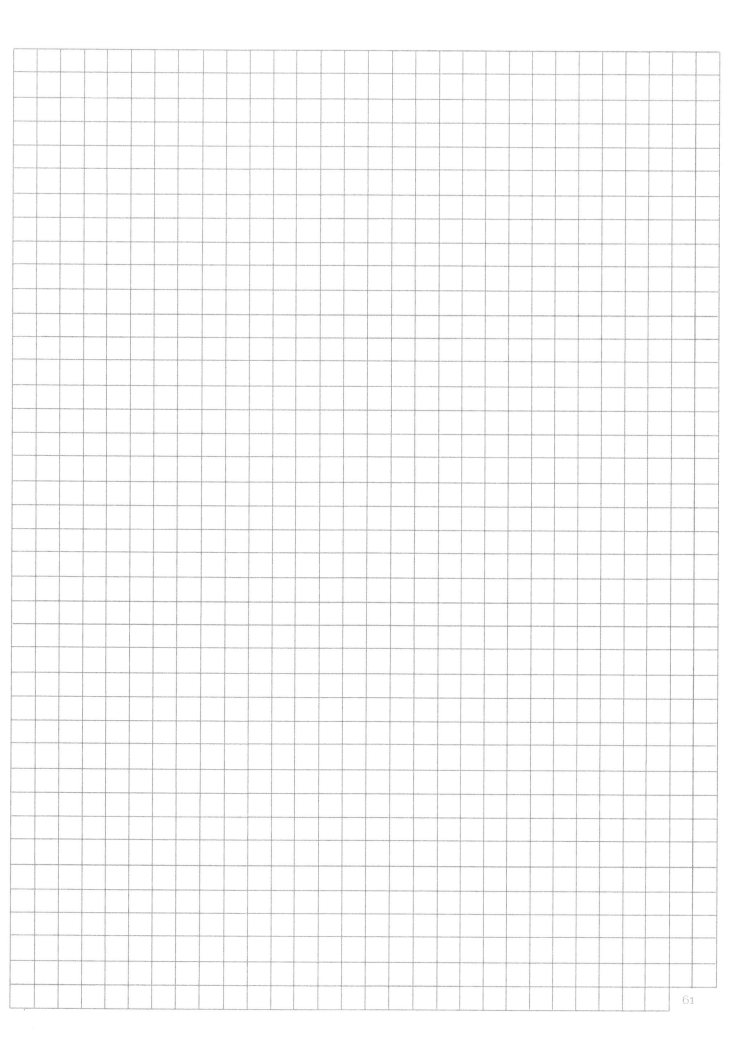

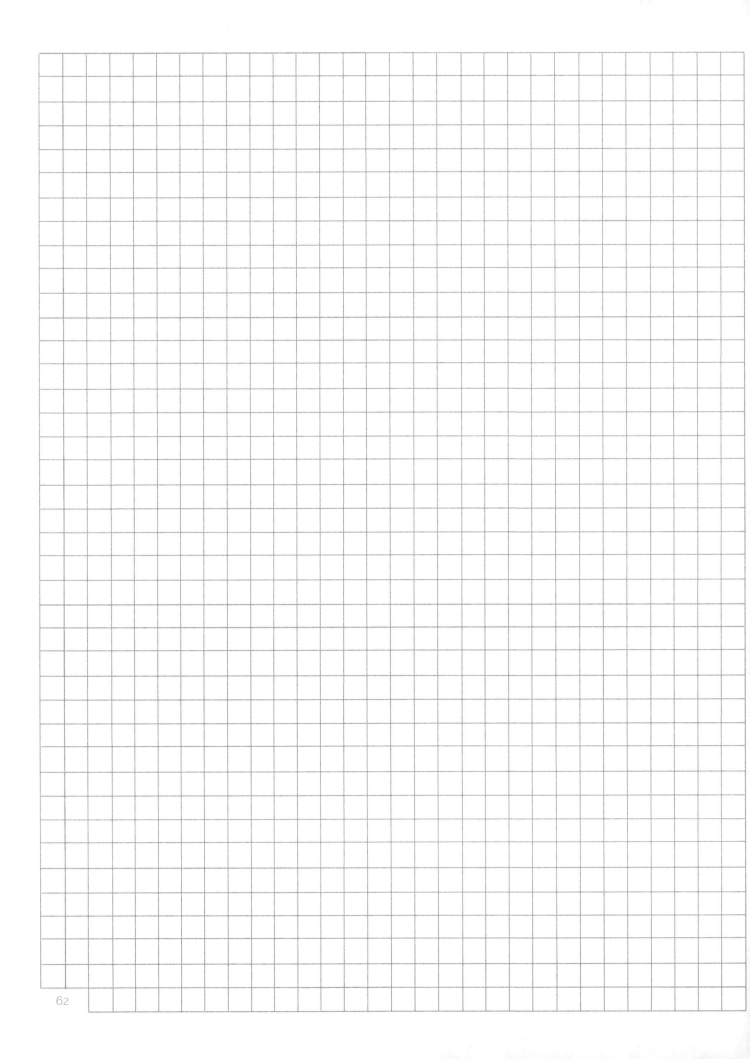

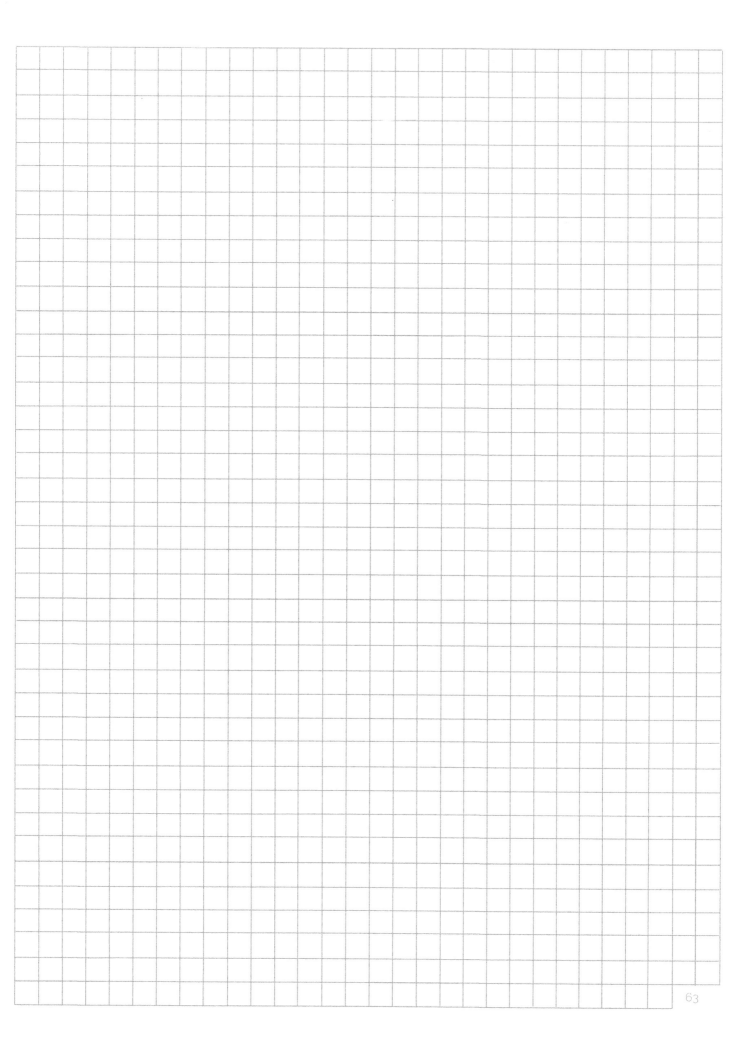

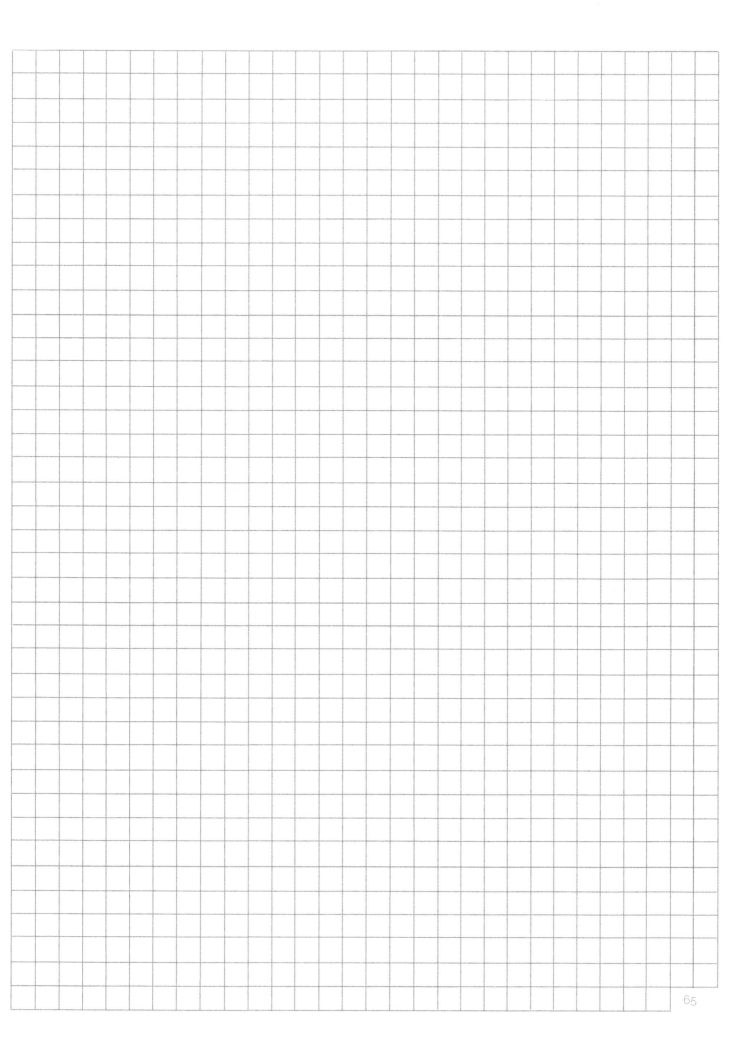

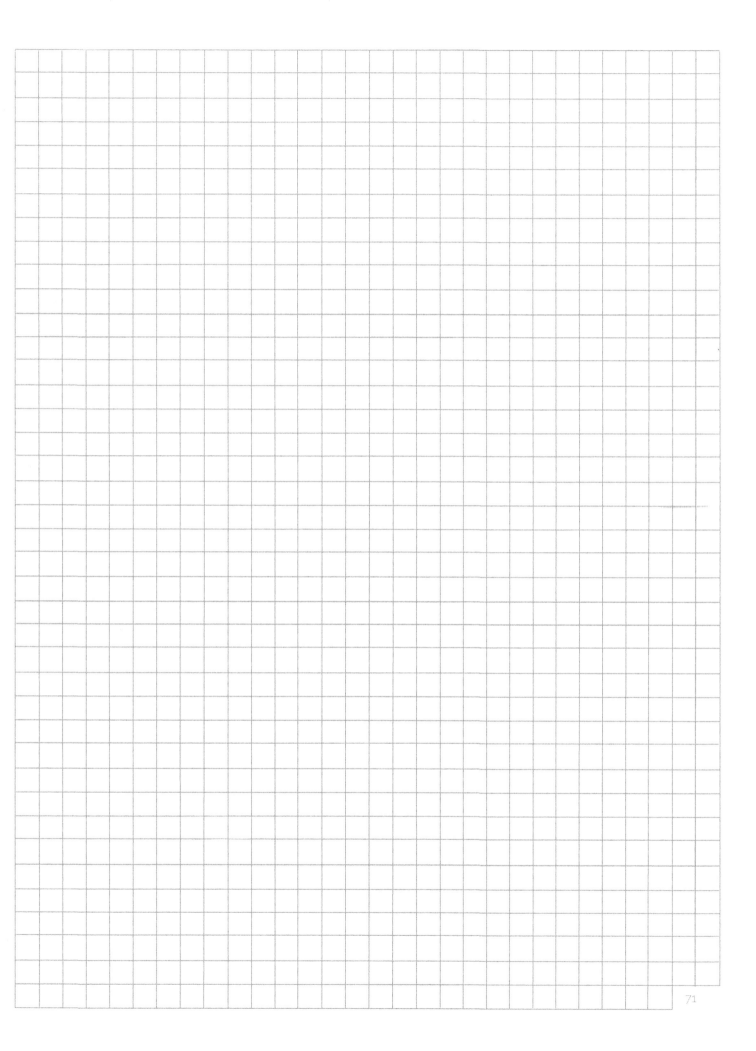

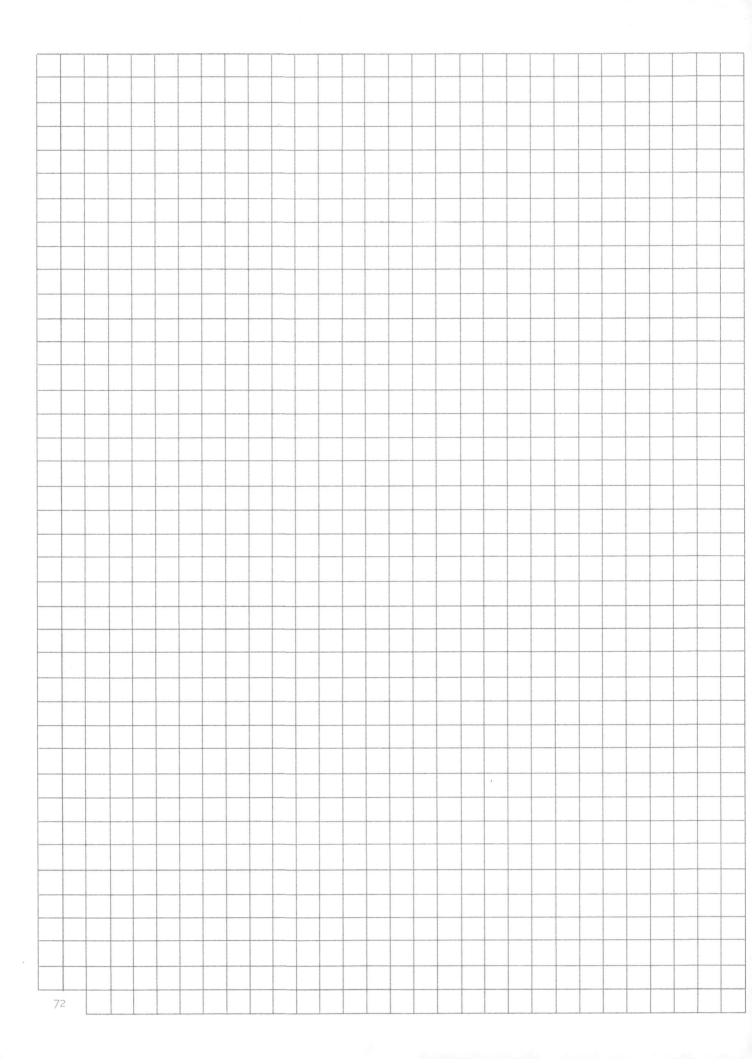

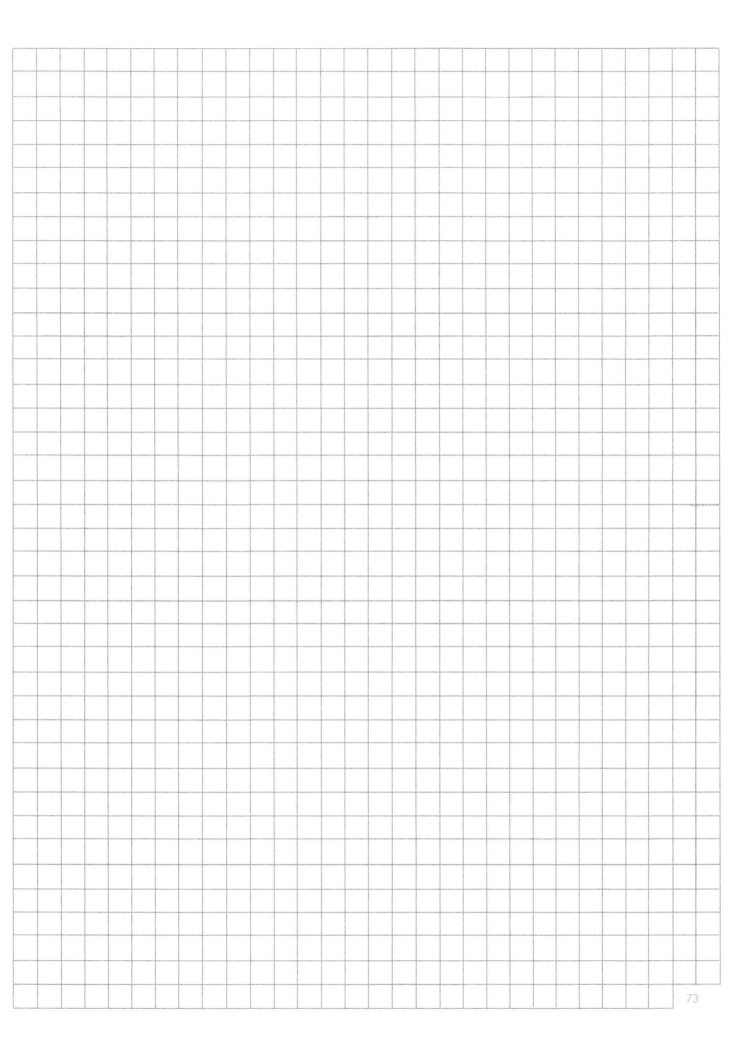

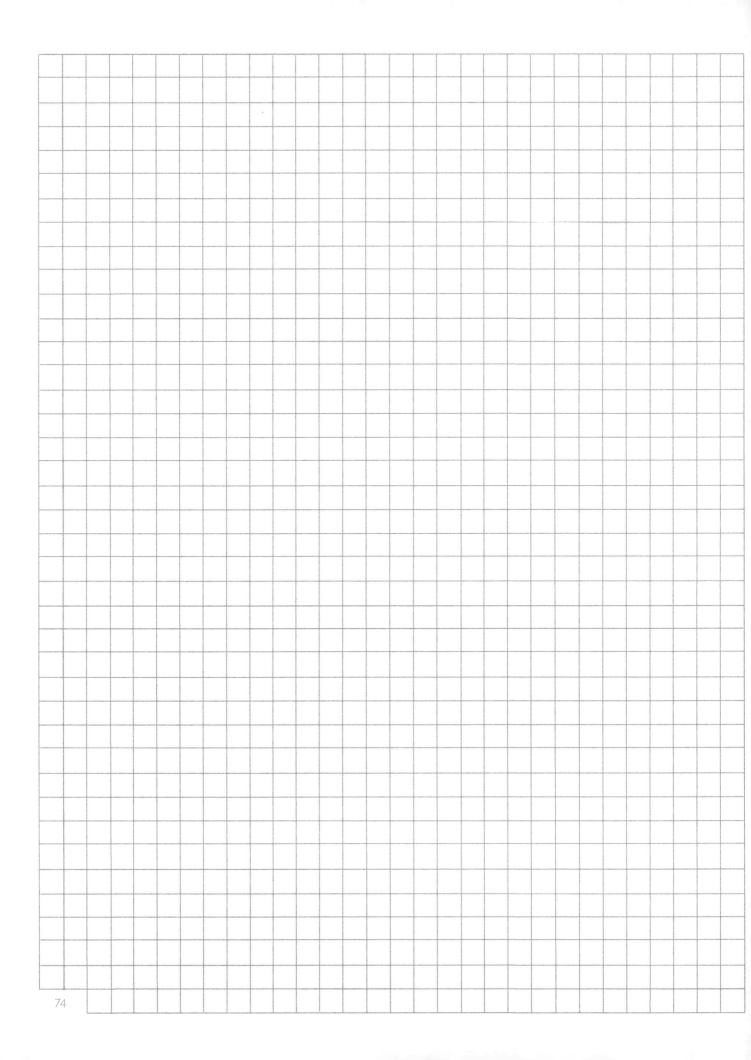

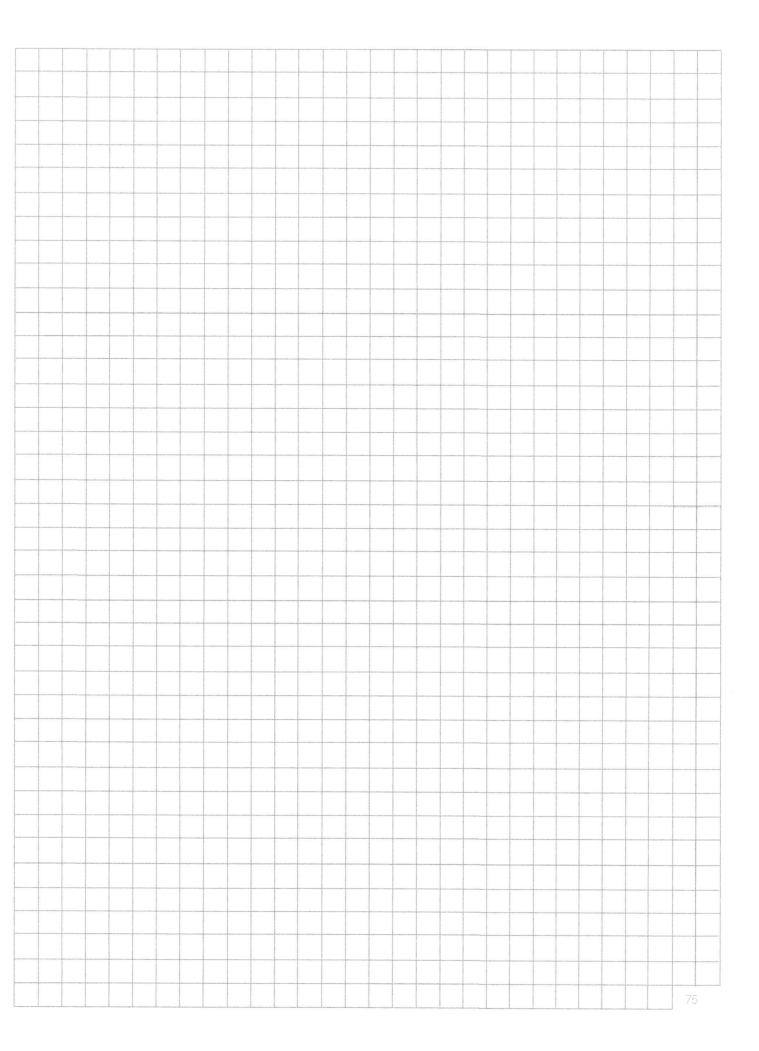

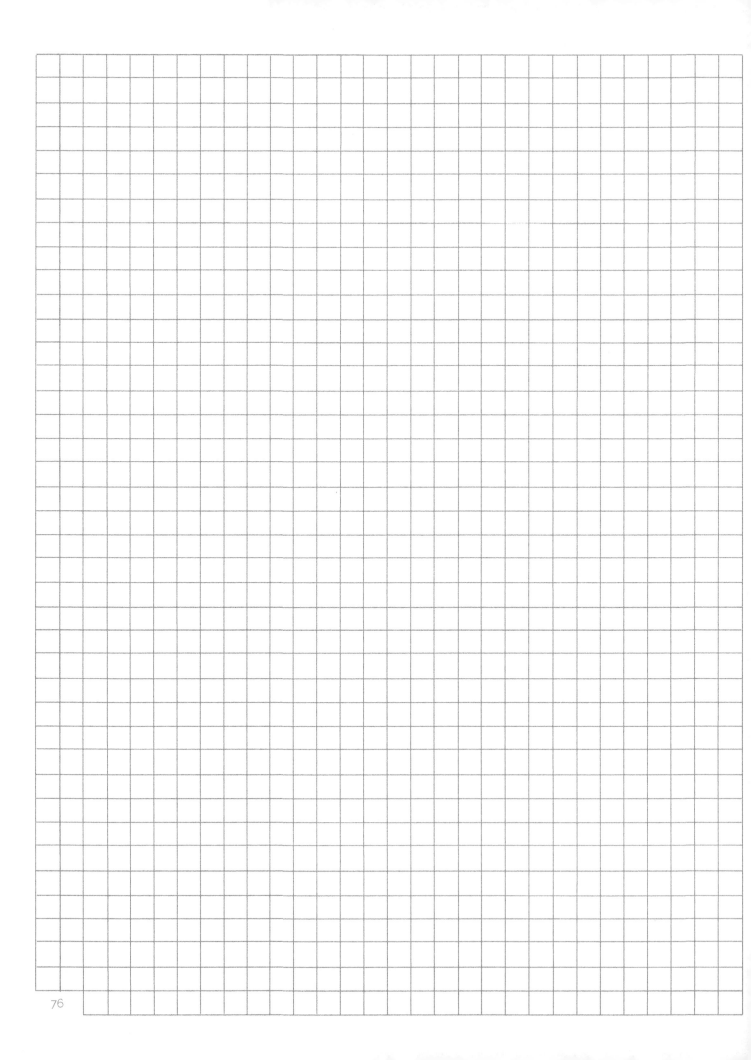

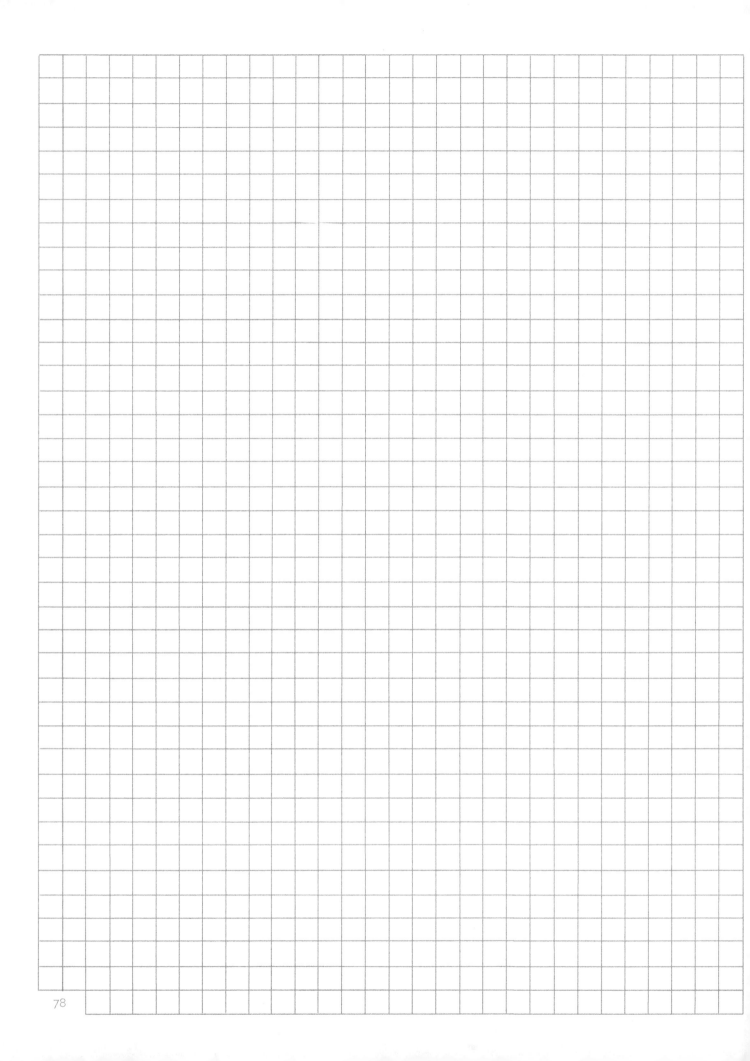

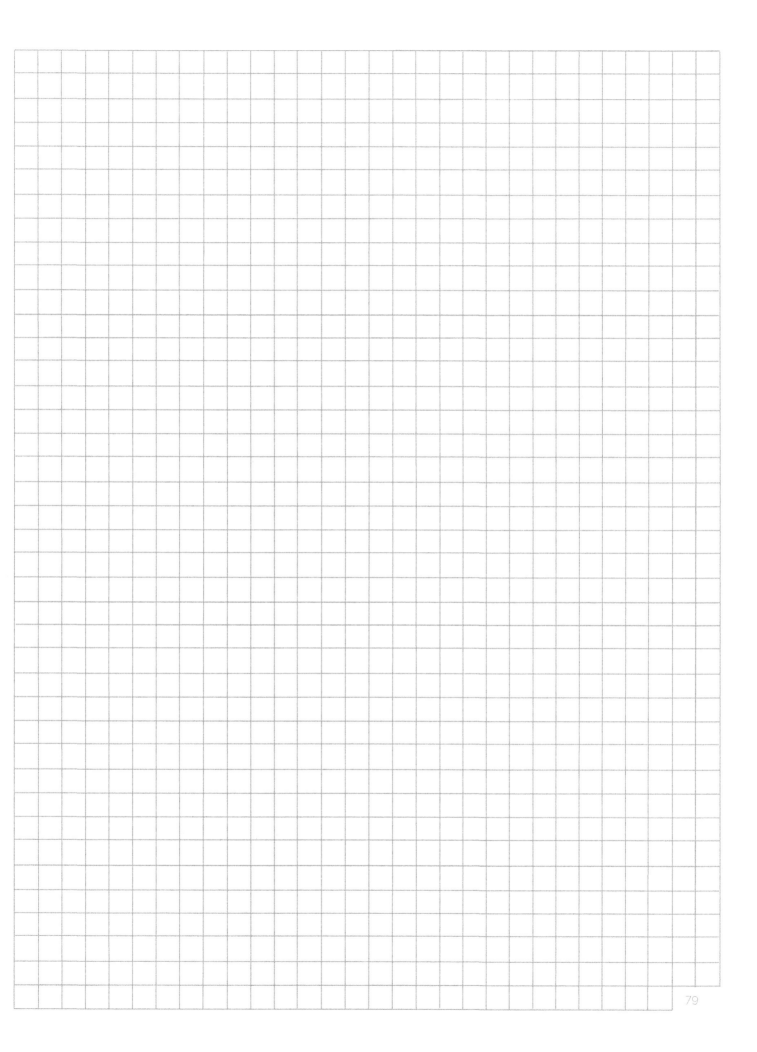

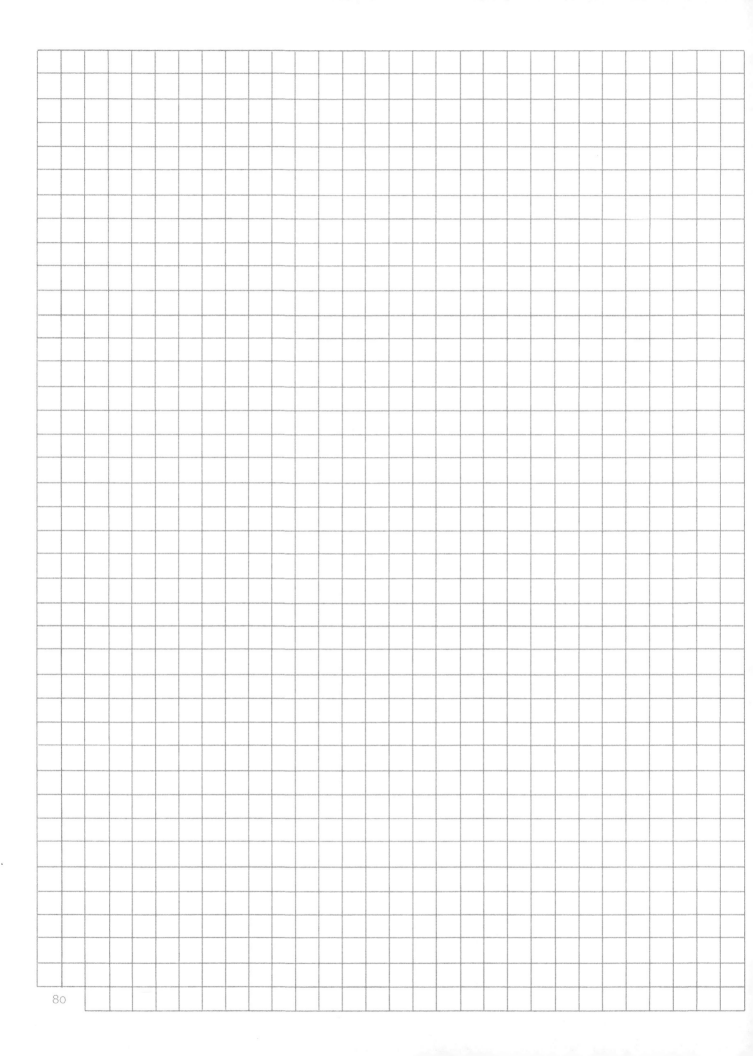

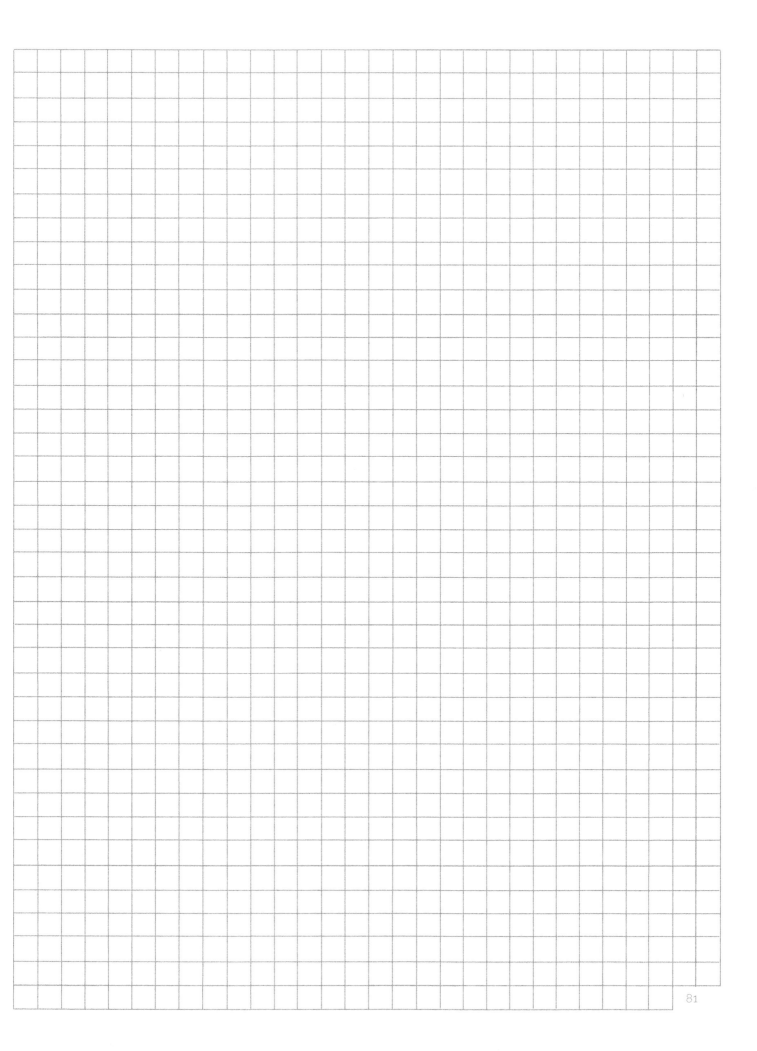

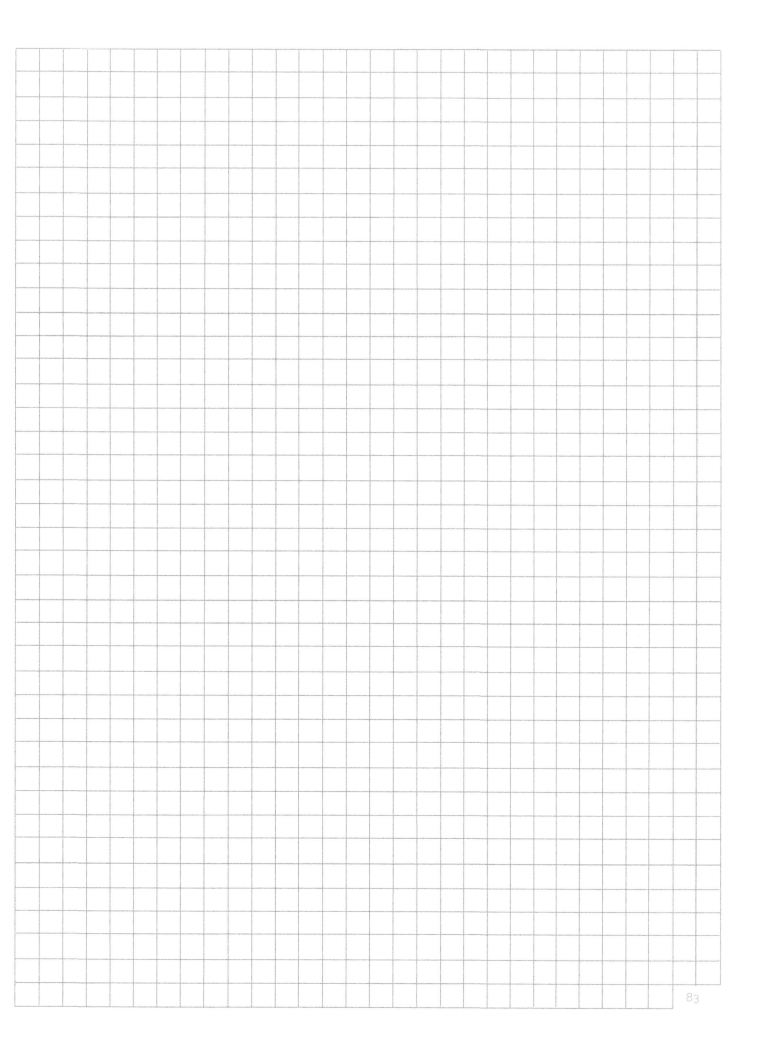

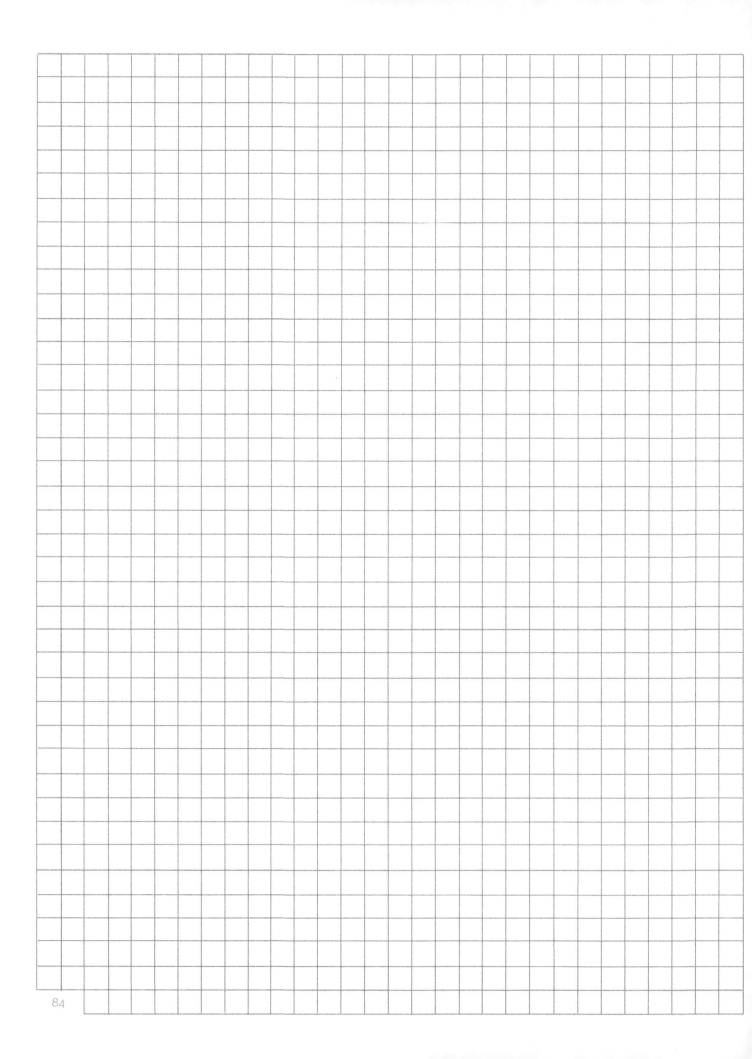

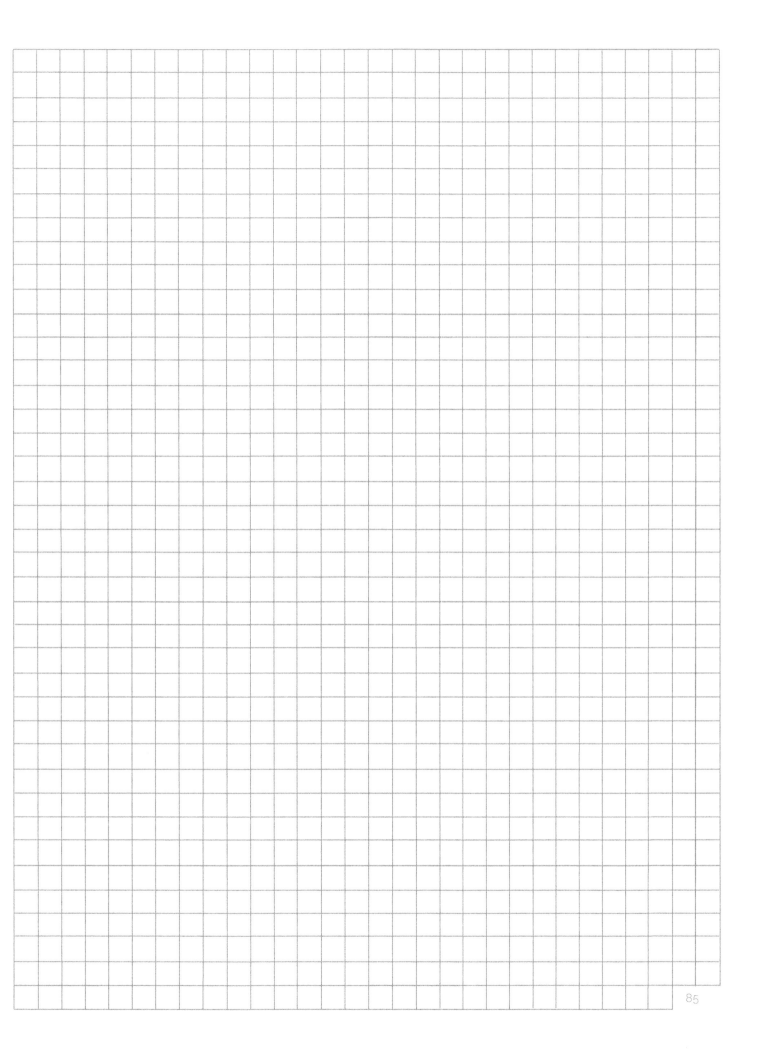

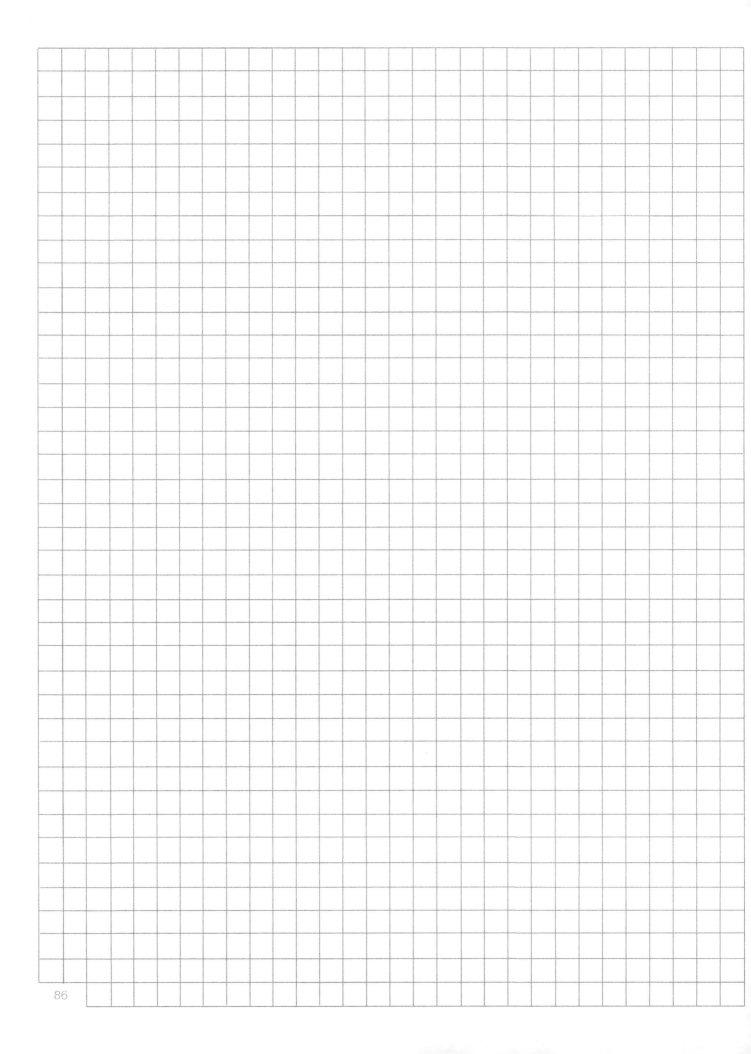

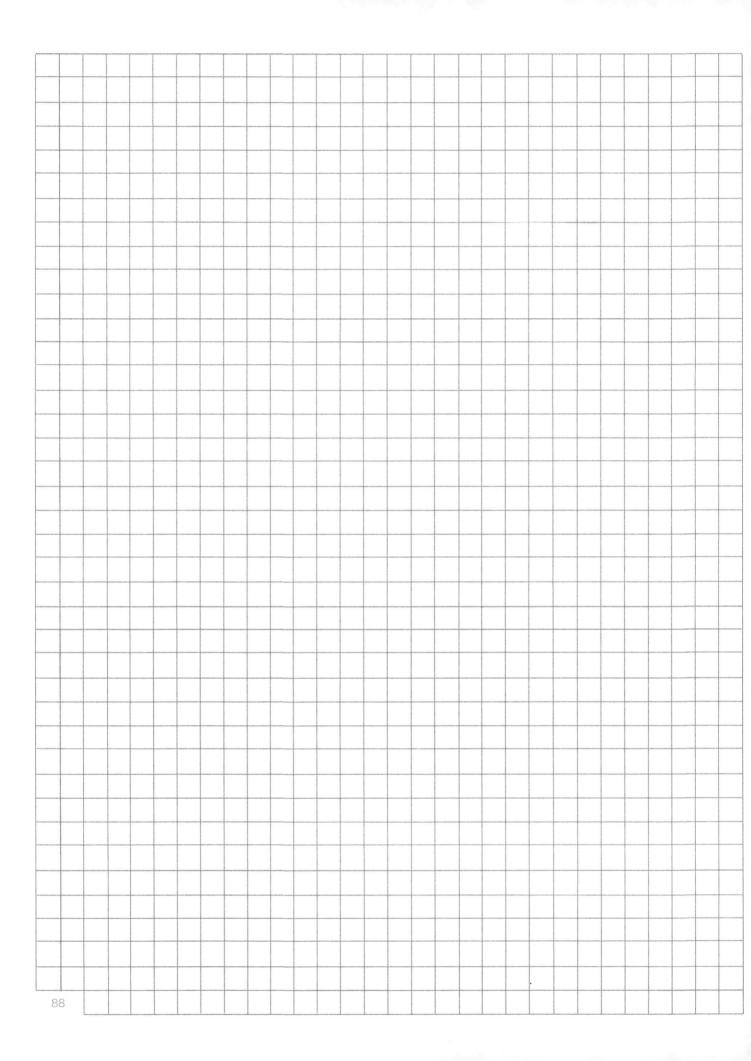

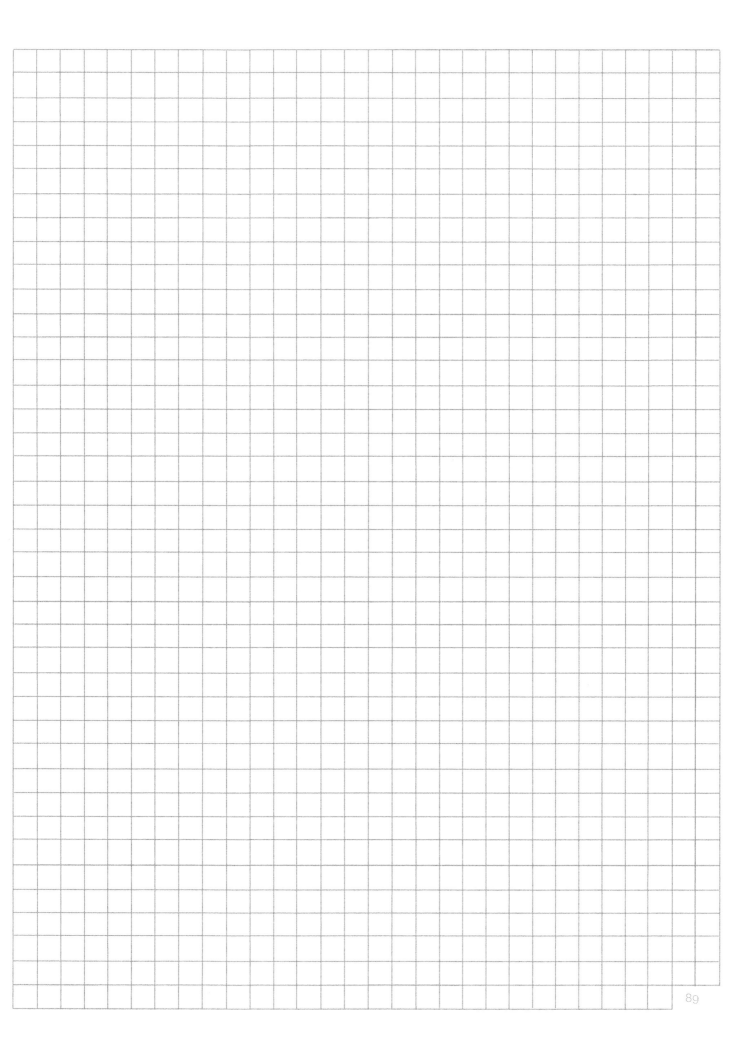

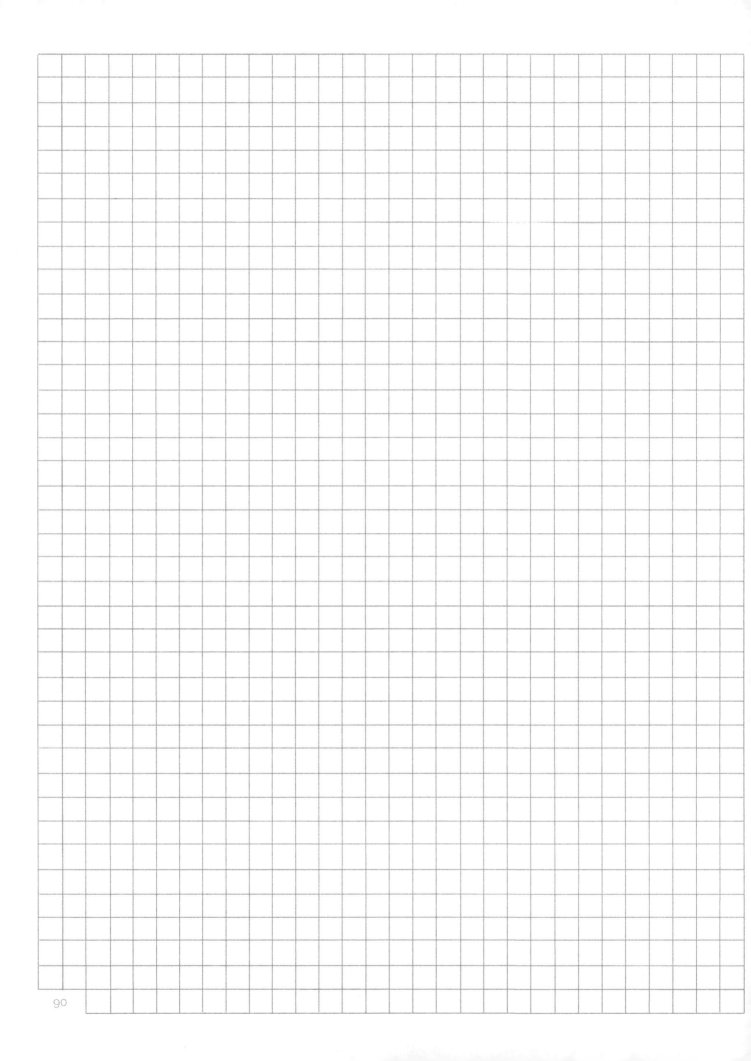

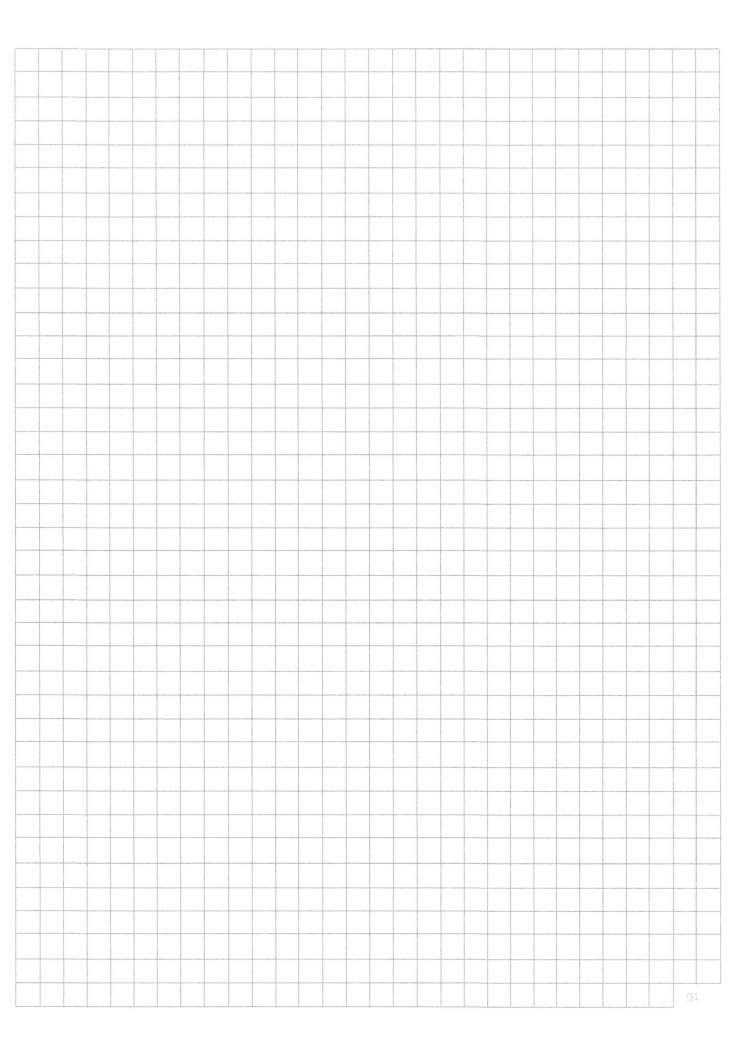

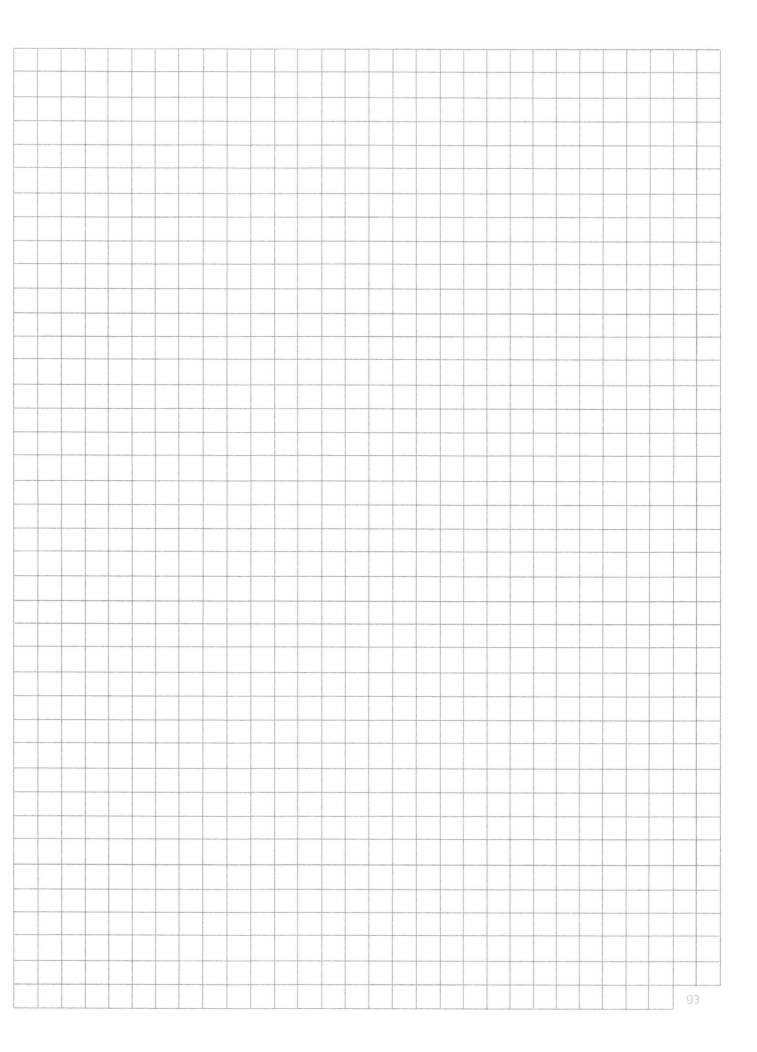

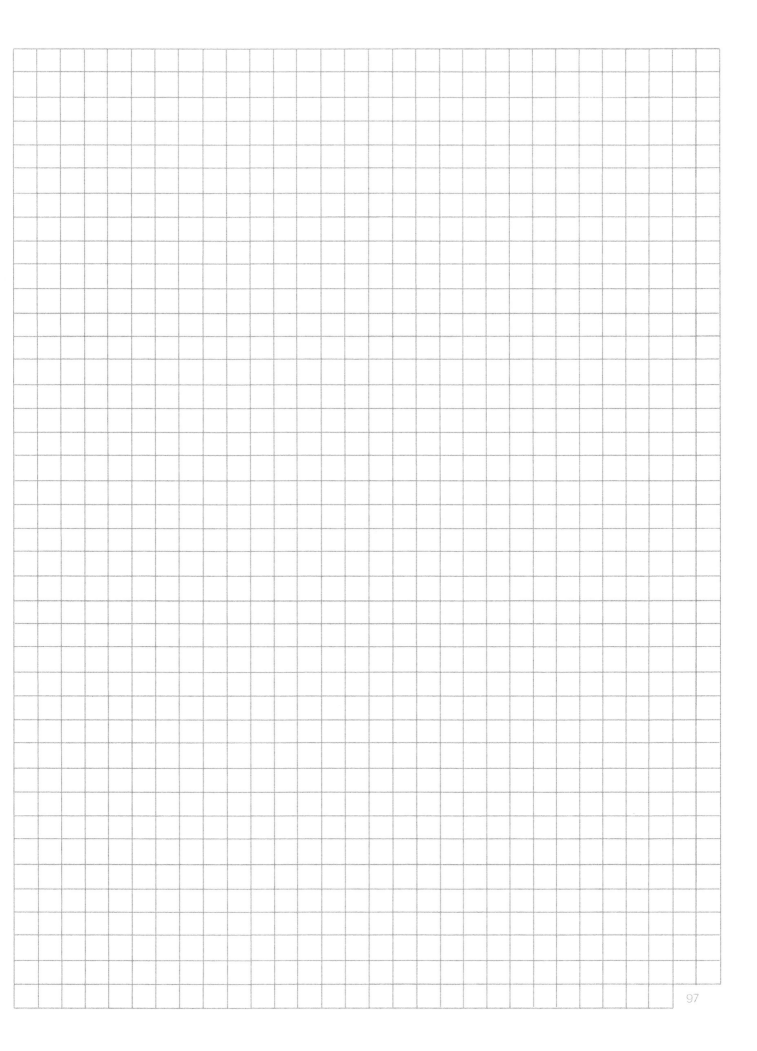

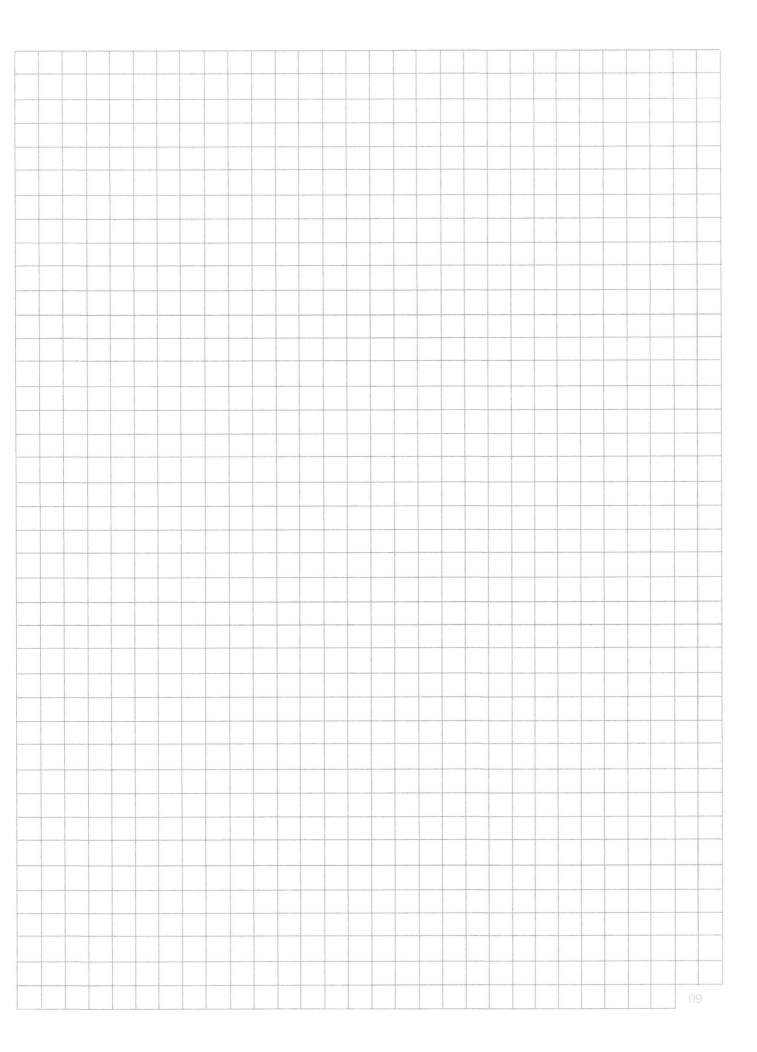

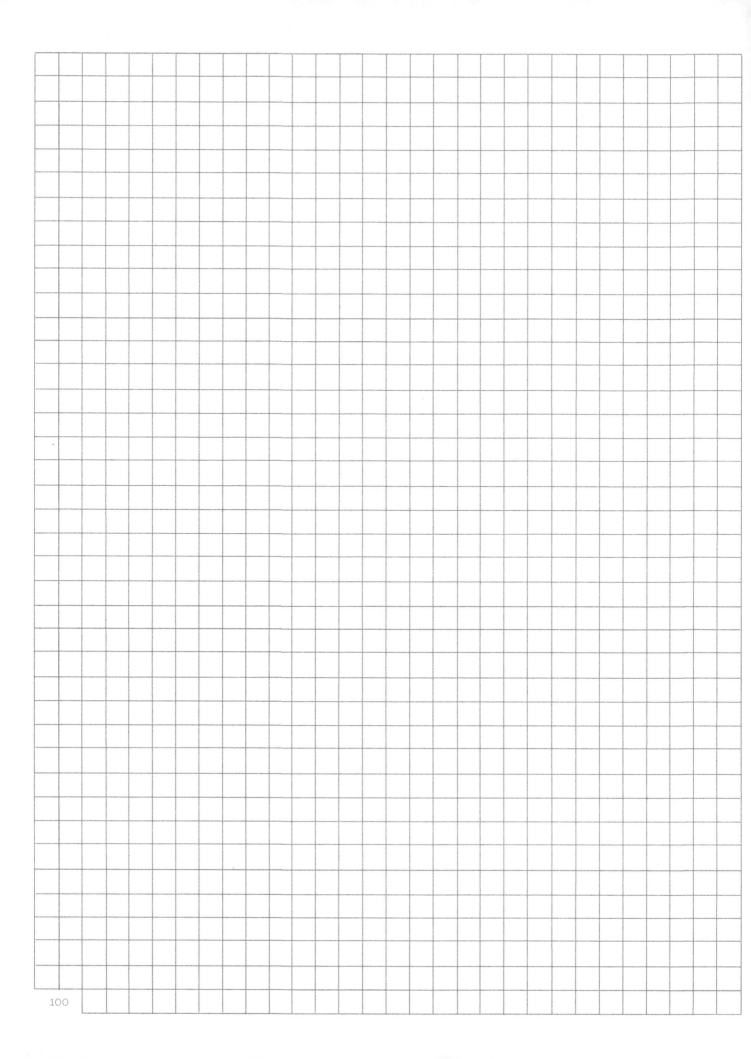

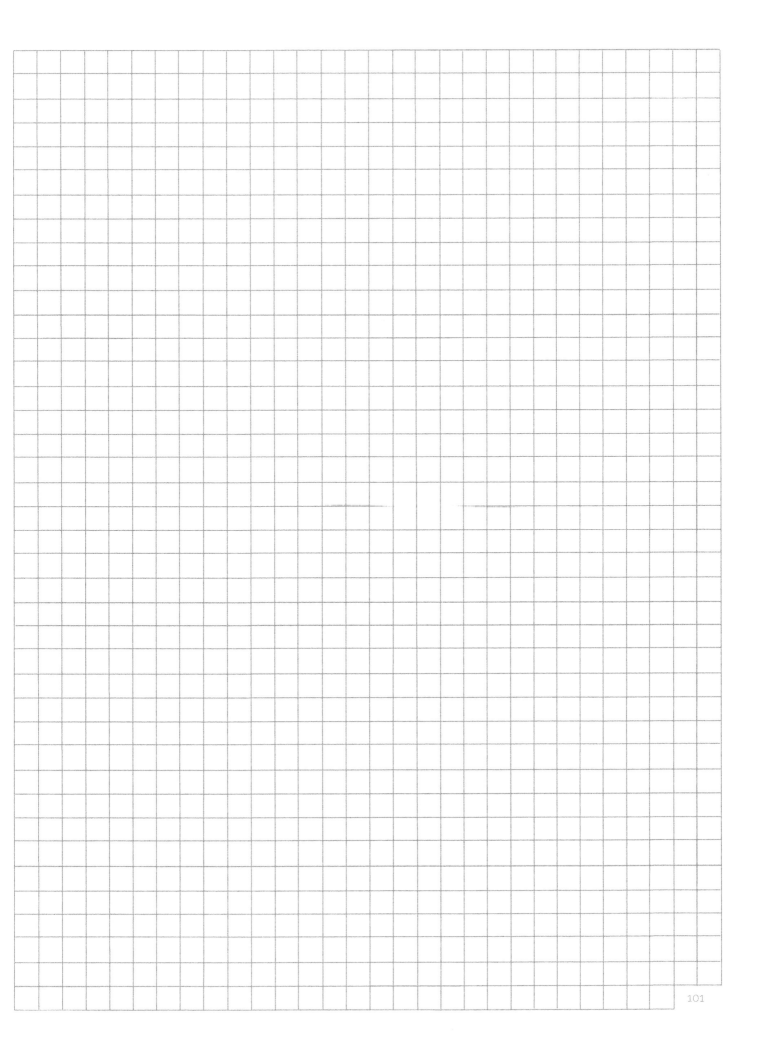

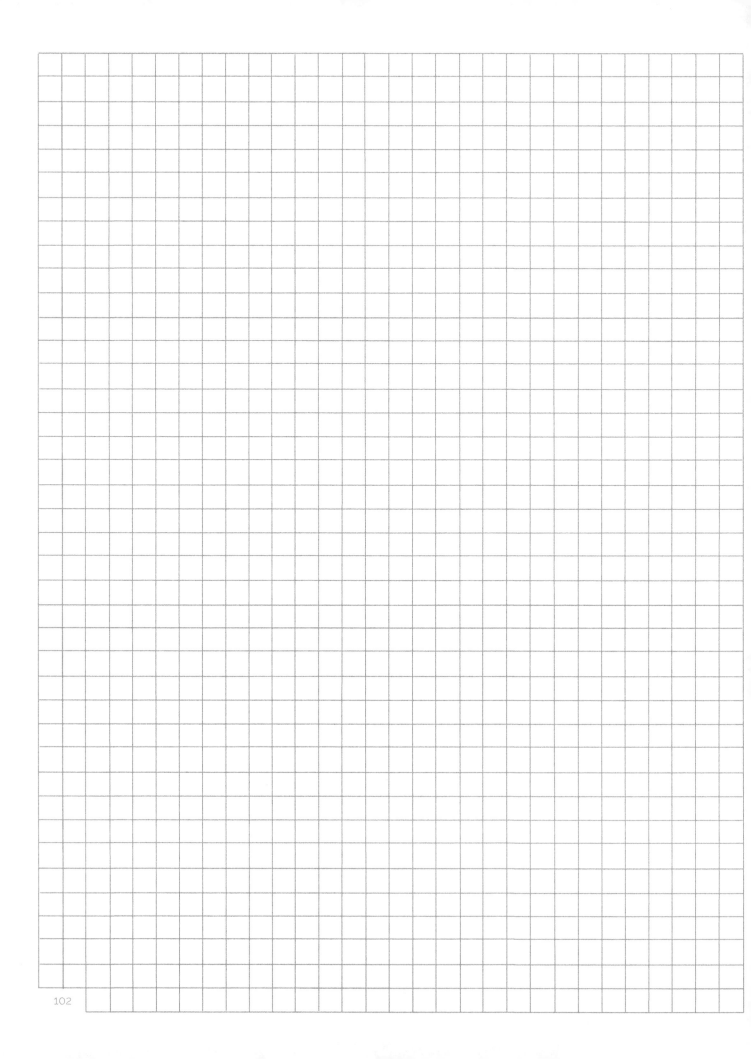

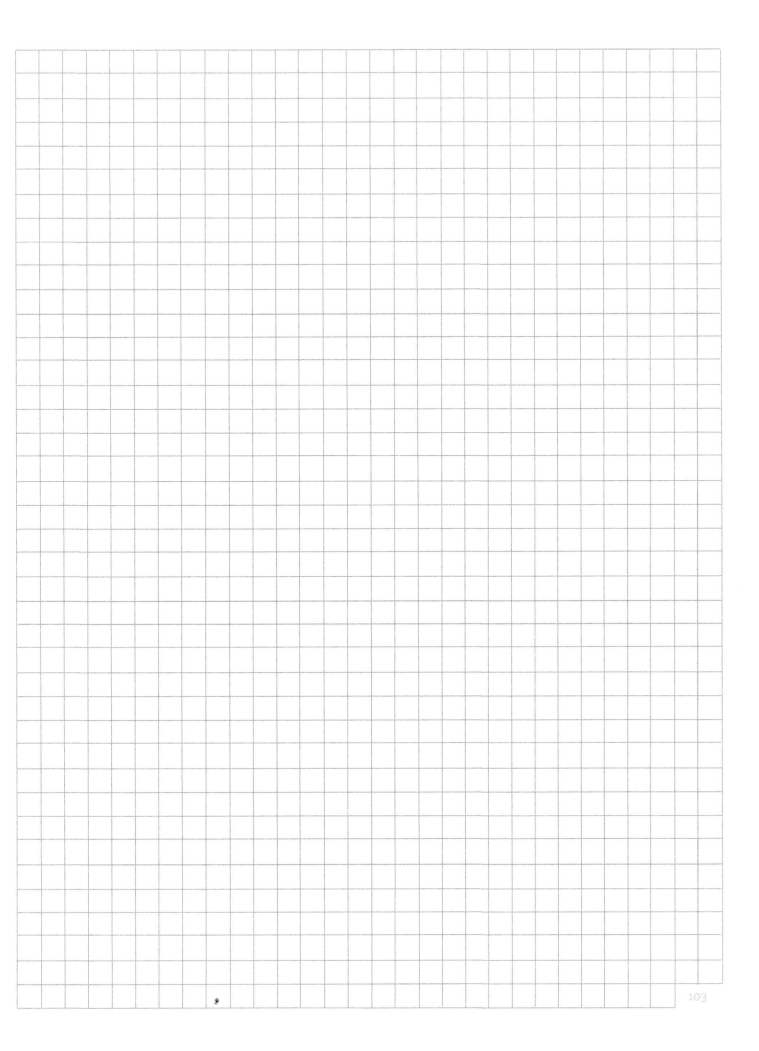

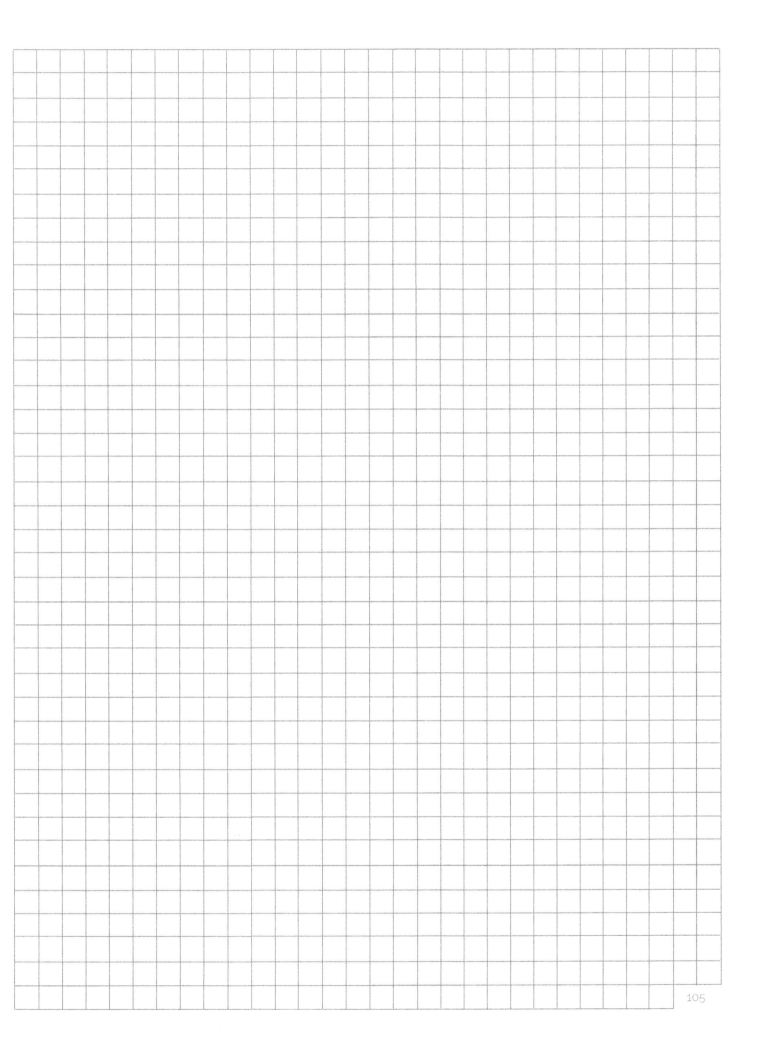

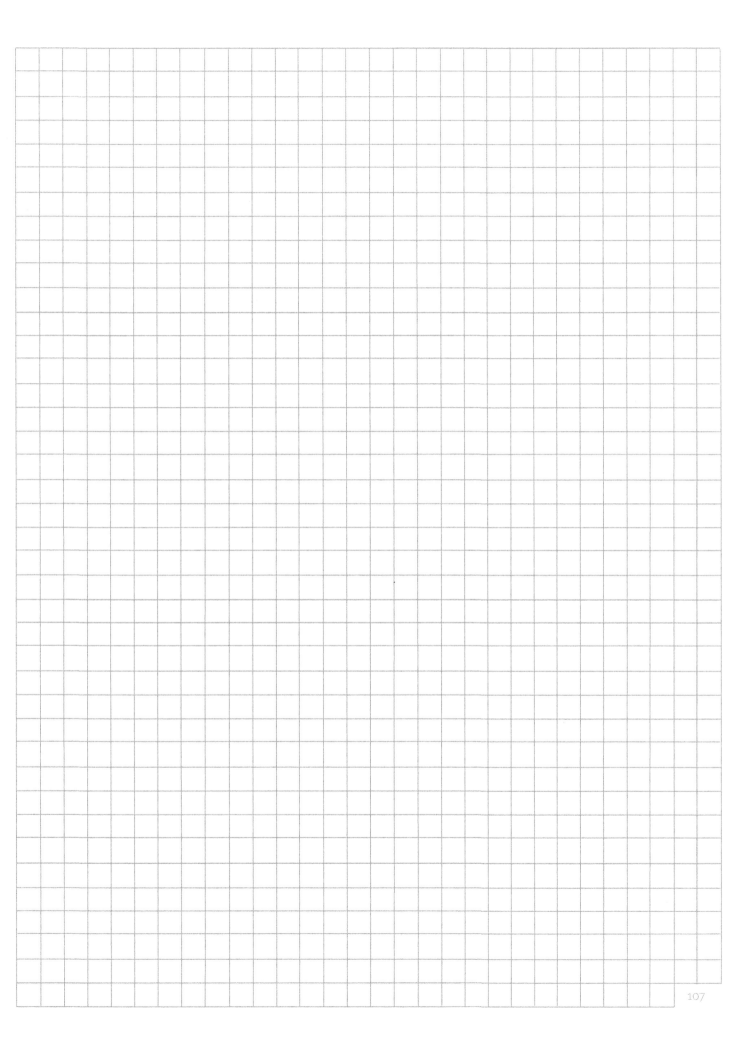

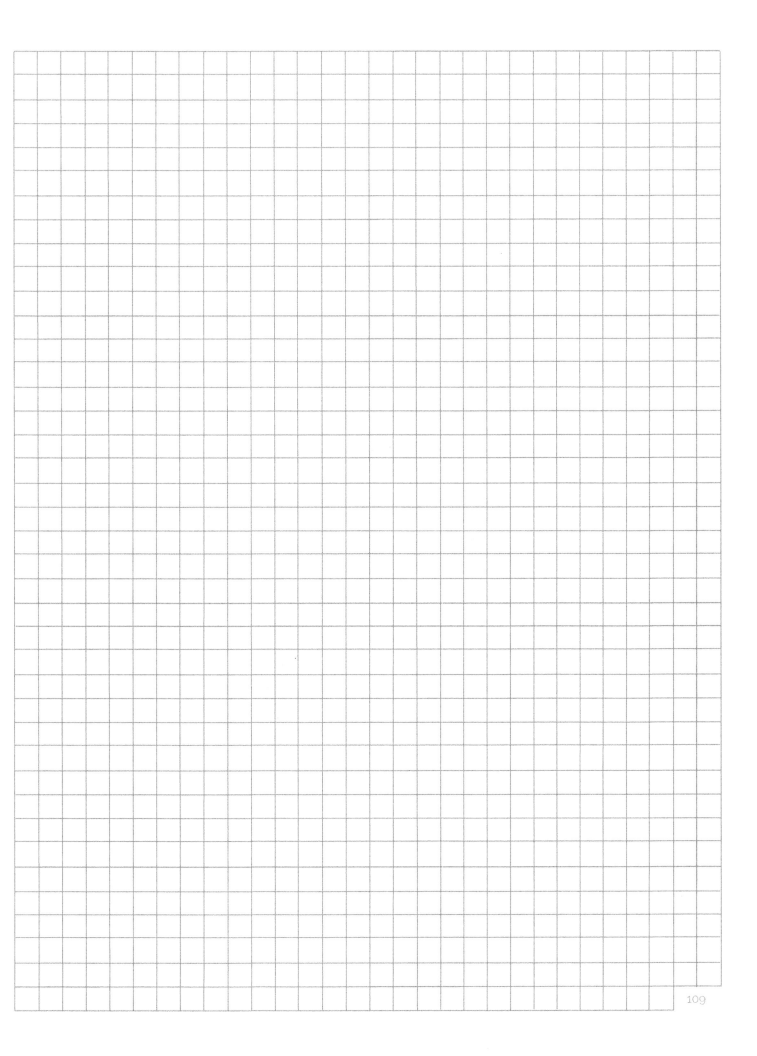

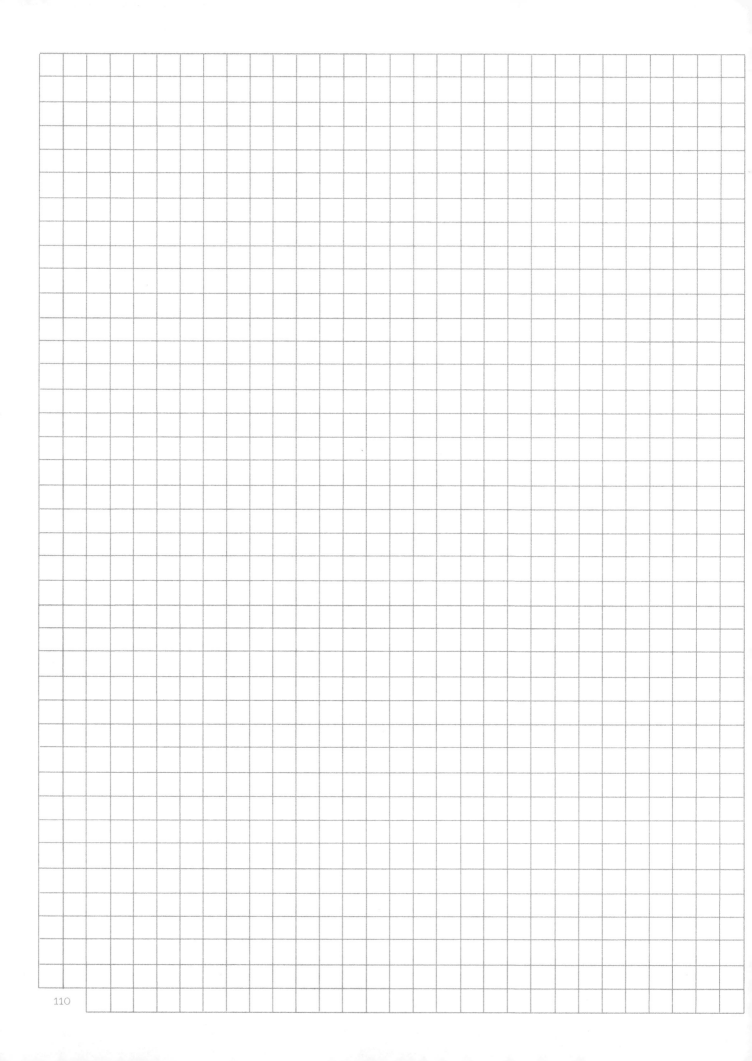

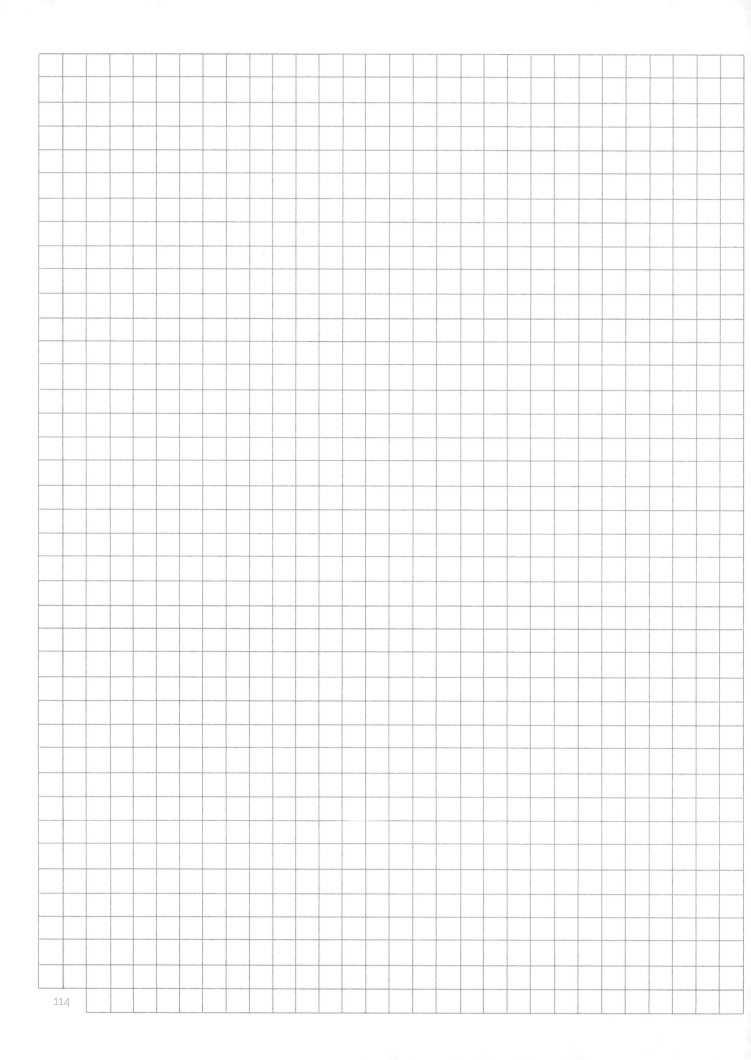

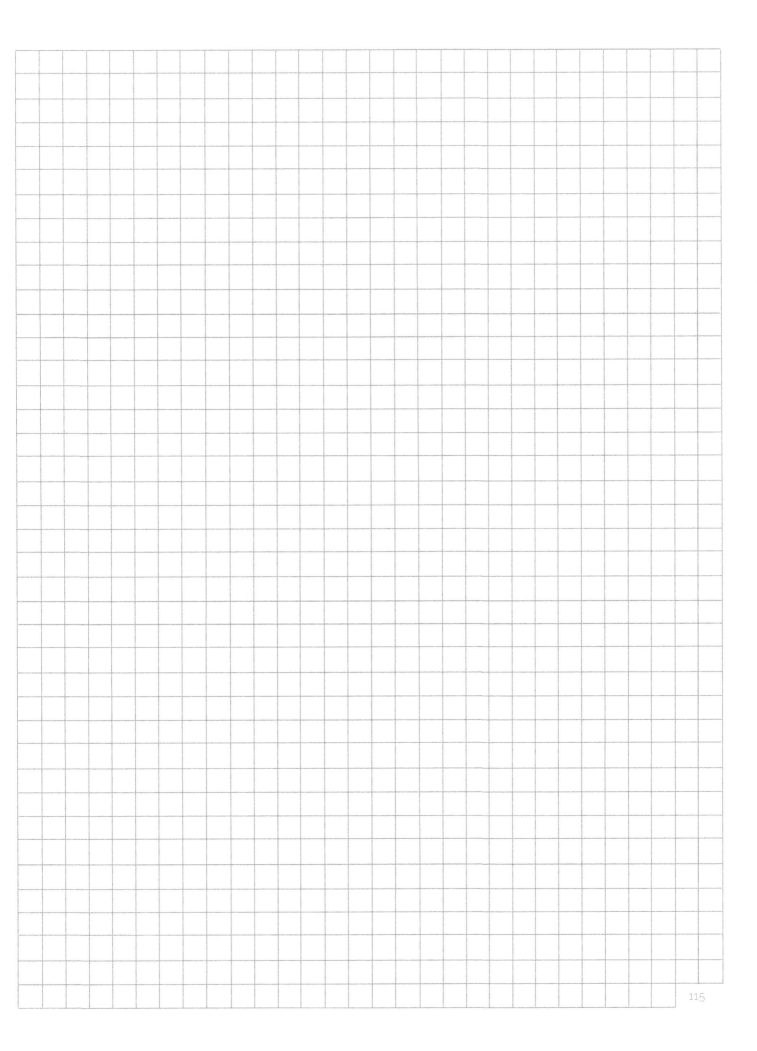

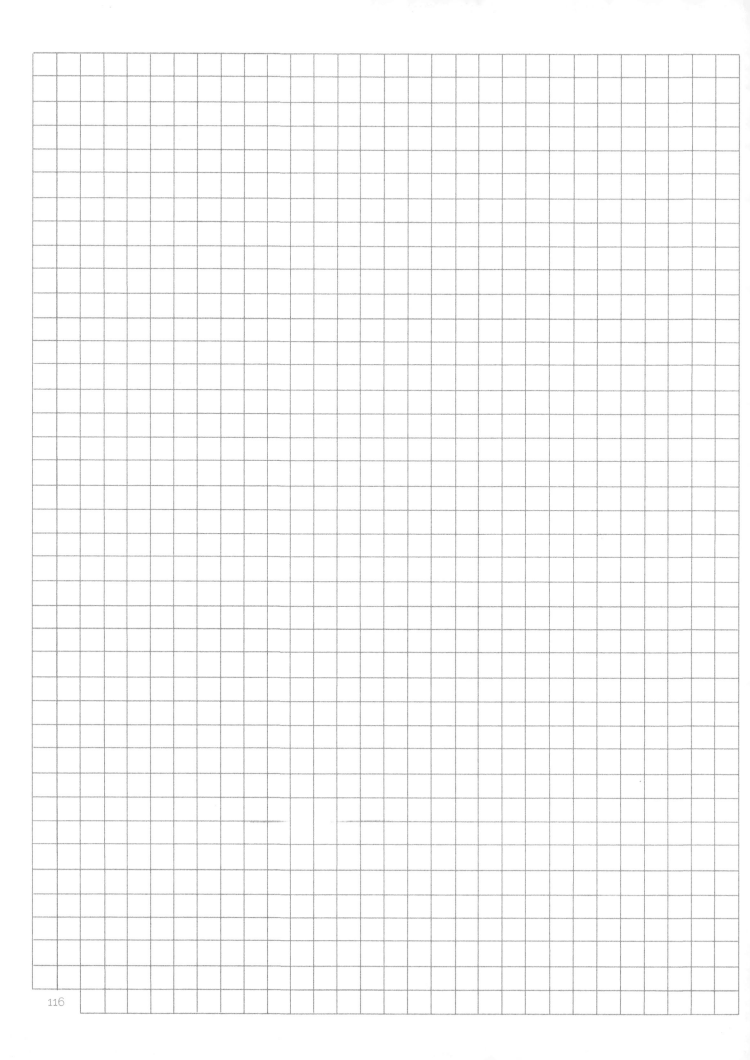

NOTES

Made in the USA
Las Vegas, NV
21 July 2024

92576593R00070